Close to Home
. . . .

CLOSE TO HOME

Revelations and Reminiscences
by North Carolina Authors

EDITED BY
LEE HARRISON CHILD

JOHN F. BLAIR, PUBLISHER WINSTON-SALEM, NC

Design by Liza Langrall
Illustrations by Debra Long Hampton and Liza Langrall

The paper in this book meets the guidelines
for permanence and durability of the Committee
on Production Guidelines for Book Longevity
of the Council on Library Resources.

Library of Congress Cataloging-in-Publication Data
Close to home : revelations and reminiscences by North Carolina
    authors / edited by Lee Harrison Child.
        p.   cm.
    ISBN 0-89587-154-8 (alk. paper)
    1. Authors, American—Homes and haunts—North Carolina.
2. Authors, American—North Carolina—Biography. 3. Authors,
American—20th century—Biography. 4. North Carolina—Social life
and customs. 5. North Carolina—Biography. I. Child, Lee Harrison.
PS266.N8C56 1996
810.9'9756—dc20
[B]   96-20229

For my girls—
Downing, Courtenay and Anna—
and their grandmother

Contents

Preface

. . . .

I used to believe that any thoughts of home worth recording had to include suppertime, rocking chairs, family gatherings, dogs and sunsets. I don't anymore. This collection has changed my mind. These intensely personal, often touching, very spirited thoughts of home include everything from barbecue to water moccasins. Not a rocking chair among them. What ties them together and makes them worth recording is the authors' willingness to be intimate, to share with us "that place in memory that stirs emotions," to tell us what they know of that place and how it makes them feel.

The places in memory in this collection come from all over North Carolina—all of the authors having lived here at some point in their lives—from Robert Morgan's "house place" on the Green River in Henderson County to Max Steele's house with a view of Bird Shoals in Beaufort. They tell us how it is to live in the South, where the light is "soft and hot and foggy." They tell us how it is to have children: "I see them on the dune. . . . Now time stands still as it does in rare moments and I know in that still moment that I am as happy as any man alive on this earth." They tell us how it feels to be a child: "In the gloaming woods and yard we drove the wheelbarrow over rocks and piles of dirt, over pieces of lumber. We were living in the new house and we had a new toy. I ran and leapt onto the sand pile and landed on my behind with a jolt. I have never felt such exuberance since." They tell us about feeling connected to, of being part of, moments of oneness, fleeting, but in memory held. They make us think of our own places in memory, our own moments of wholeness.

My place in memory is not here in North Carolina but three hours south, a small town in South Carolina where my ninety-year-old mother still lives in the house I grew up in. Built as the guesthouse for one of the neighboring antebellum estates, the house sits unassumingly on a hillside among acres of longleaf pines. Its face having been lifted many times, it bears little resemblance today to the prefab bungalow that arrived in a Sears box around 1915. Still, it retains its lopsided, creaky-board, understated charm. It fits into the hill just fine.

One of the things I liked best about our house was the dirt road at the bottom of the hill. Forever gullied and rutted by hard Southern rains, the road was the object of much conflict within the town when I was young. Everyone on the road who mattered—everyone, that is, except the Millikens, who lived at the end of the road and were fussy newcomers—wanted the dirt road to remain as it was. They set about the signing of petitions about every other year. I was always relieved when word came down that we'd have our road awhile longer. And I was pleased we weren't newcomers or friends with the Millikens. That road is still dirt today. My hunch is petitions are no longer necessary.

Another thing I liked about where we lived was that the Buckley family lived next door. Even though they were only winter residents, everyone knew who they were, so I was always pleased to give directions to our house. Besides, Mrs. Buckley made being Catholic not so weird. She went to Mass every single morning and always sat in the front pew. I figured the closer you sat to the altar, the holier you were. I assumed the closer I was to Mrs. Buckley, the holier I was. And I lived next door.

The town itself is a seductive little place, country-road chic and down-home casual all thrown in together. It's filled with lovely old homes set back on wide, tree-lined streets. Tall, two-story piazzas abound, along with columned porticos. I always thought about how it would be to live in one of those houses, to sit on the upstairs porch and sip tea. I always thought that's the way life should be, me on my porch sipping tea.

There's a special softness about things in this town, my children speak of it still when we go back. The climate is mild, the air gentle, and when spring hits it's as if a magic wand has been waved over the town. Growing up here, you assume this is the way spring is. It seems you're forever scornful of other attempts to get it right.

People who come to Camden for the first time think they have discovered some kind of nirvana. I don't feel that way because I've known it too well for too many years. For me, the soft air is tinged with sadness about the way things were here and the people I knew. But I like that it's home, and the little house still ours, and I still feel a tug each time I drive away.

My father came to Camden to run the polo in 1940. He played a rich man's sport without being a rich man, but he played it so well that it didn't matter. I was hugely proud of his polo skills, even though as a child it was an odd thing to say your father did. But he always seemed happy and loved to laugh, and he liked me a lot and taught me to dance. A week before my twentieth birthday, he died while playing in an indoor polo match. Those who came to console said it was a grand way to go, the way he would have wanted. But I didn't think it was grand. I knew better than they. I knew he would have wanted time to grow old, and a chance to dance at my wedding.

My mother came from a family that valued good taste, good looks and good breeding. Fortunately, she had all three. With a wing and a song, they have seen her through ninety-plus years of a good and happy life. She has never had a bad-hair day. Highly social, elegantly aloof, she approached motherhood in a somewhat formal, highly polished fashion. Still, my sister and I were well tended, went to proper boarding schools and always spent the summers in places less humid.

I don't ever remember sitting on my mother's lap. It's not that she didn't love me, it's just that touching wasn't her thing. But my first child, when she was two, hadn't gotten that message. I came home one day to find my little girl sitting on her grandmother's lap. The die was cast. She for whom motherhood was a job without frills launched into a grandmothering career that blossomed with the wind. And it was as if she had known how all along.

Inroads made by the first grandchild were only broadened by the second. Now there were two little girls to take over the room I had called mine so many years before. And they found any excuse to spend the night there: somehow the sheets were much softer, the baths bubblier, the pillows fluffier, the sleep sounder. There was no chaos there.

By the time the third little girl arrived, her place at the table was already set. They had fine dinners on starched linen cloths in the dining room, lit only by candles. Dressed in matching nighties, they ate artichokes with hollandaise, drank apple juice from fine crystal and learned about finger bowls. They sang camp songs that my mother had learned years before, songs about the White Mountains and Squam Lake and evening time. They memorized poems by Edna St. Vincent Millay. They skinny-dipped in the dark. They ate ice cream with chocolate sauce. And no one seemed concerned at all that Mrs. Buckley had long since died and her place next door been sold.

"There is no question," as Louis Rubin, my Hollins professor of years gone by, says of Charleston, "that being born and growing up [there] was the experience that has exerted the greatest formative impact upon my imagination—on the way that I think and feel." Though we moved away many years ago, Camden is that place for me—the one that nourished me, then allowed me to move on. As in the stories in this collection, that place in memory brings us (as Max Steele describes in "The House of Their Childhood") to a place where we see our life against our destiny and know something of its meaning—epiphany, revelation, a coming together, for a moment, feeling close to home.

Lee Harrison Child

Acknowledgments

. . . .

One of the grand good pleasures I had as editor of *NC Home* magazine was traveling the state, visiting houses and gardens and galleries and studios of all imaginable shapes and sizes in every conceivable corner of North Carolina. What made the job unique was the people—not only the ones who built the houses and designed the gardens and painted the canvases, but those who wrote about the people who painted and designed and built. The homeowners, architects, artists, shopkeepers, photographers, chefs, gardeners, writers—all of these played a part in creating a portrait of North Carolina that we who worked on the magazine looked on as something special.

Contributing to this portrait—and one of my favorite parts of the magazine—was the "Writers Write" column that appeared each month, original pieces by some of North Carolina's finest writers. The only directive they received for writing the column was that it have something to do with their own experience of living in North Carolina. What emerged on those pages were rare and wonderful revelations, funny and fragile and heartrending. Up front and personal. Full of grace. Too good to let go with a single sighting, those stories were the inspiration for this collection.

It is to those writers—the eleven whose work first appeared in the magazine and the ten others whose work would have, had we endured—that I owe the greatest gratitude. Generous of both time and talent, they made my job a privilege from day one. I thank them for this, each one.

David Kinney, publisher of *NC Home* during its all-too-brief run from 1992 to 1994, made the magazine happen in the first place. His vision for the publication and his upbeat, unerring support kept us going as long as we were able. I'm grateful to David for this, and for introducing me to managing editor Lisa Davis, who made us all look good almost all of the time.

When I approached John F. Blair, Publisher, with the eleven magazine stories in hand, Carolyn Sakowski with enlightened foresight welcomed them and wanted more. Her steady guidance and enthusiasm throughout have been, for me, invaluable. Thanks, too, to Steve Kirk at Blair.

I send my thanks always to my mother, Virginia Watts Harrison, who was especially sorry when the magazine folded because she had to send pears instead of *NC Home* to her friends for Christmas. Thanks to my sister VV, friends all around, my girls all three and Tom—the most creative man I know.

ANGELA DAVIS-GARDNER

The Ghost Marks of Stairs

The house where I grew up—British

general Cornwallis's headquarters during

the Revolutionary War Battle of Guilford Courthouse—has recently been made into a museum. The architectural layerings of two hundred years, including the additions made by my family, have been stripped away. All that remains is a small log cabin, the core of the house we lived in and which, though unseen, fired our imaginations. Grateful though I am to the citizens of Greensboro for preserving the eighteenth-century structure, saving it from developers who saw the land as a prime spot for an office park, it is a shock to see the house of my childhood memories deconstructed.

The contours of the land, however, are intimately familiar to me, and the trees: the maple that stands by our erased driveway and beside which, my historian father Burke Davis thought, some of the Scottish Highlanders who fell in battle were buried; the sycamore in what used to be the pasture where our Shetland pony grazed; the Osage orange tree, which dropped its odd, pimpled chartreuse fruit onto the tennis court every fall; and, in front of the cabin, the ancient cedars, a few of which have fallen since I left here some thirty years ago.

I was nine the day we first saw the house, my brother five. Newly arrived in Greensboro and living in an apartment in town, my family one summer afternoon drove out into the country toward Guilford Battleground Park for a picnic and one of my father's educational tours. But my parents were also house hunting, in a desultory way. As we headed up New Garden Road near the park, my mother cried out, "Oh, I wish we lived there!" My father slowed the car and we all stared at the little clapboard house perched on a hill behind cedars: though dilapidated, it had, with its tin roof and dormer windows, a peculiar charm. Then we noticed the small For Sale sign in the yard; my father turned the car up the drive.

The house was unlocked; we walked right in. There was an odor of dampness and age. The living room was empty except for a shabby grand piano in one corner. There was a huge picture window gashed in one wall. "We'll have to fix that," my father murmured. My mother sat down at the piano and began to play Chopin, the keys only slightly out of tune.

During the process of buying the house, my father learned the uncanny coincidence of his already having written about this place in his historical novel *The Ragged Ones*; beneath the clapboard was the cabin Lord Cornwallis had commandeered as a hospital for his troops during the penultimate battle of the Revolution. It was a turning point in the war, as my brother and I were often to hear, a Pyrrhic victory for Cornwallis, who at one desperate point in the battle fired upon his own men, consequently so debilitating his already weakened army that it was defeated at Yorktown.

With the help of a carpenter who lived nearby, my parents began recovering what they could of what we called Cornwallis House and at the same time making it habitable. The refurbishing went on throughout the ten years we lived there. The crucial years of my late childhood and early adolescence are connected in my mind with the sounds of sawing and hammering and planing, as the house continually evolved around us. In the living room, the low ceiling was taken down and the original beams exposed; the pine mantel piece was stripped of paint and sanded to a fine glow. It became an invitingly cozy room, especially at Christmas, with a huge cedar we cut in the nearby woods filling one corner and Christmas cards strung across the mantel. A dining room and modern kitchen were added; the lean-to at the back of the house was made into a screened porch, where a ping-pong table was installed. The happiest changes for me were the additions made to the sides of the house; at last, I could move from the cramped loft into a real bedroom with twin beds, a dressing table, and, nearby in the hall, a phone I could drag inside the room, to talk behind my locked door.

Each time there was an excavation, we searched the ground for signs of the battle. Though few relics were found, my father made the most of them. "Now look here, kids," he'd say, holding a brass button stamped with the words *Treble Gilt, London.* "Off a redcoat's jacket for sure." The Seventy-first Highland Regiment formed in our yard and surely brushed right past our back door, he told us. From the house and the nearby countryside—with my father as tutor—my brother and I learned about the Revolutionary War in an extraordinarily vivid way; at the same time, our own histories were beginning imperceptibly to mingle with that other history.

We swam in a pond whose source was Horsepen Creek, where the British were first fired upon. When it snowed, we played fox and hounds with my father all over the several square miles of battlefield, always pausing at the statue of General Greene and other historical markers. Home again, warming ourselves with cocoa by the fire, we were invited to picture Cornwallis sitting here—in front of our fireplace—nursing his wounded arm and brooding over the cannon fire that killed his own men. My father told me that the dark splotches on the floor of my loft bedroom were said to be bloodstains from the wounded soldiers quartered there; while this did not occasion, as I recall, bad dreams, it did give me excellent material, when friends spent the night, for ghost stories about the soldiers buried in the yard and about Cornwallis, who always returned to the scene of his crime one night a year at midnight, always on *this* particular night.

I began to write stories in this house, too. I put out a handwritten publication called *Cornwallis Weekly*, which was, according to the masthead, "issued every few days," though the one extant copy may have been my only effort. Inside are stories about a wounded bird, a cake stolen by a hungry dog (and grouchy Mama Davis's reaction), ads for housework chores, and numerous pasted-in photos, including the editor's fifth-grade school picture. The lead story is "Literary Lettie Home from Mexico," about my parents' friend Lettie Rogers; the caption notes her absent-minded expression, common to novelists. I had reason to know: not only were both my parents writers, there were always other writers about the house, creating a literary atmosphere that must have been infectious—certainly part of the reason my brother and I both became writers ourselves.

But there were other reasons, too, most of them having their locus in this house. Greensboro has grown out around the place now, but when we lived in it, there were fields and woods all around, with just a few other widely scattered houses. I remember the solitude, the deeply quiet, dark nights, the hours spent reading. On the pony or my bike, I roamed the countryside, sometimes peering into the cars parked on Lovers' Lane or boldly going down small, winding dirt roads to seek out the nudist colony rumored to be in the vicinity.

The very peculiarity of the house had much to do with shaping me as person and writer. Though I treasure my memories of its uniqueness now, during my adolescence, endured in the conformist fifties, the house was a source of embarrassment. "You actually live here?" more than one friend asked, seeing the place for the first time. Not only was it "out in the sticks," the house, even in its more elegant later phase, with a brick-veneer front and two clapboard wings, was—that most damning word—*different*. Part of this had to do with the distinctive shape of the house, the fey angle of the roof and the dormer windows—nothing like the brick ranch houses that had begun to spring up in town.

Today, the preserved cabin is in a small, green oasis called Tannenbaum Park, after the chief financial supporter of the preservation; it is surrounded by shopping centers and condos with names like Lincoln Green and Cornwallis Mews. Often, I am drawn back to the site, to peer through the cabin's small, leaded windows—newly added—and, when the house is open to the public, to step inside what used to be our living room.

Our furniture is gone, of course, and the shelves of books, but I do recognize the exposed beams and the pine mantel piece my parents restored. The fireplace has been rebuilt, however, the handmade bricks my parents had laid removed in favor of more authentic stone; when the hearth was torn up, one preservationist who worked on the cabin told me, they found my name written in the cement beneath the bricks. The boxed-in staircase to the loft has been replaced by steeper steps that were reconstructed, I learned, from ghost marks of the earlier stairs found in the closet below. It was in that closet—gone now—that we used to keep our Scrabble and Monopoly games.

Upstairs, in the loft where my brother and I had our bedrooms the first years in the house, there is nothing, expect pure space, to remind me of what was here. Even the dormer windows—through which my brother and I had to crawl on fire-drill days and then shinny down a cedar pole held by my father—are gone. I have to close my eyes to summon up the rose-patterned chair, the canopy bed, the radio playing Perry Como or Eddie Fisher while I anxiously studied my preadolescent face in the mirror. It was in this room that I began to consider the future. "March 22, 1952," I wrote on a piece of paper. "Twenty years from now where will I be?" That paper, much creased, almost illegible, is still in my jewelry box at home.

Outside the cabin are newly constructed outbuildings, jarring to me, though no doubt valuable to the tourist: there's a detached kitchen, a forge (with a resident blacksmith on weekends), a large barn, circa 1820, which was moved from another part of Guilford County and which stands where our tennis court once was.

I think of the so-called historical additions as fictions, not only in terms of my history but of that battle which is reenacted on the site every March 15. The outbuildings are an attempt to interpret, in preservationist lingo, a typical eighteenth-century homestead. Though restorers made every effort to discover what buildings were here, it is impossible to know exactly. All history, even written history, is part fiction. I first learned this from my father. As carefully researched as his fiction and nonfiction accounts of battles here and elsewhere are, it took a vivid imagining on his part to bring them to life.

On my most recent visit to the cabin, I sat on the newly constructed bench that encircles the Osage orange tree while my twelve-year-old son roamed around the cabin. I love this peculiar tree and am so grateful it was saved. I used an Osage orange tree (and a fictitious tree house in it) as the center of my novel *Forms of Shelter*. Though the novel is not in the usual sense autobiographical, the tree is an emblem to me of this place—a place I write from, though not directly about.

My son was quickly bored by his tour of what he calls "the old place"; we went to the nearby visitor center and looked through the exhibits. He hefted a musket and tried out the stocks. We put our heads above cardboard cutouts of an eighteenth-century woman and boy, looked in the mirror, and laughed at our reflections.

In the gift shop (The Guilford Sutler), my son tried to talk me into a musket, finally settled for a clay pipe. I looked around, slightly depressed by the collection of stuff—the little flags, potpourri, pottery birdhouses, colonial paper dolls—newly minted souvenirs of a generalized notion of eighteenth-century life.

By the cash register are postcards of what is now called the Hoskins House, after Joseph Hoskins, who built it in 1778.

"I used to live there," I tell the cashier, holding up one of the pictures of the little log cabin.

"Oh?" She smiles politely but looks confused; her expression says she surely has misheard.

> **Angela Davis-Gardner** writes fiction about the places that haunt her—in Nova Scotia and Japan, as well as North Carolina. Her latest novel, Forms of Shelter, was a hit in France and has just been reissued in this country.

LEE SMITH

. . . .

Blue Heaven: A Chapel Hill Memory Album

May 1965

We leave Hollins at 10 A.M., six of

us crammed into the car, Mary

Withers driving. "My Girl" is on the radio. Some of us know our dates; some don't. I don't. He is an SAE, but I can't remember his name. I am already tired. I have been up for hours, ironing my clothes, ironing my hair. At Martinsville, we stop for gas and road beer. We sing along with the radio. Now it's "Help Me, Rhonda," by the Beach Boys. We are getting real hot in the car because it doesn't have any air conditioning, but we can't open the windows much because we would mess up our hair. I keep trying to remember my date's name. We stop in Danville for more road beer. "Ticket to Ride" is on the radio. Now we are in Chapel Hill; now we are pulling up in front of the fraternity house; now all these boys are standing up and walking out to the car. Oh no. What is his name? *Oh no.*

MAY 1965

In formal clothes, we walk right up the middle of Franklin Street, giggling and singing. Doug Clark and the Hot Nuts played at the party. My date passed out, but now I have another date. He is from Scotland Neck, which I find hysterically funny. The sun is coming up. I carry my shoes. It was some party.

JUNE 1966

Summer School. I sit on the grass near the Davie Poplar, books thrown down beside me. A soft wind blows my hair. I stretch out my legs. The boy puts his head on my lap. He wears a pastel knit shirt, pastel slacks, loafers. He looks like an Easter egg. But he is a golfer. I sigh languidly. I am in love.

AUGUST 1966

It is a hot, smoky cafe, the smoke barely stirred by the sluggish overhead fan. The backs of my legs stick to the sticky wooden booth. This conversation is very intense; it is the most intense conversation I have ever had, and also the most beer I have ever drunk. It is very, very late. This is a *great* conversation, I can't believe how significant it is. He leans across the table toward me. He pounds on the table to make a point. With his other hand, he touches my knee under the table. He is a member of the SDS. We light more cigarettes. I am in love.

AUGUST 1967

It is raining, and we have been walking for hours, in a light, fine drizzle that jewels the edges of everything. We are soaked through. We stop to sit on one of the gray stone walls that are everywhere in Chapel Hill. We kiss. I run my finger along the jeweled stone. This time, I am really in love. Later, much later, he will move to Chicago, taking my life-size painting of the Supremes and breaking my heart. Eventually I will recover. He was from Connecticut and talked funny.

JUNE 1973

Finally I move to Chapel Hill with my first husband. I have always wanted to live here. So has everybody else who ever went to school here, and once school is over, many of them can't stand to leave. So everybody who comes to work on our house has a Ph.D. in something: the plumber's degree is in philosophy; the painter is a historian. I am embarrassed to have all these educated people doing manual labor on my house. I offer them coffee and cake. The carpenter listens to opera while he builds bookshelves. I have second thoughts—are we cool enough to live in Chapel Hill? I won't let the children play with the gun toys while the workmen are here, so they won't think we are rednecks.

SUMMER, MID-1970S

A party on Stinson Street, probably Anne Jones's house. Everybody I have ever known has lived on Stinson Street at one time or another. Stinson Street has constant parties, constant yard sales. Anyway, at some point during one of these parties, I go outside to get some air and wander across the street to Leonard Rogoff's yard sale, where I stand transfixed before a chest of drawers with a mirror attached to the top of it. I stand before the chest and look into the mirror for a long time. The mirror is tilted so that I can see a tree, the moon, my face. *Oh no*, I think. *This is really my life, and I am really living it. Oh no.* I remember thinking that then, on Stinson Street.

LATE '70S, EARLY '80S

I sit on the edge of the Rainbow Soccer Field, where my kids are playing Rainbow Soccer, which is noncompetitive. You can't yell anything like "Kill 'em!" or "Stomp 'em!" This is hard for some parents. My son Josh is playing center forward. I am writing a novel.

I sit at the Chapel Hill Tennis Club, waiting for my son's match to start. This is my son Page. He's real good. I am writing a novel.

I sit in a wing chair before the fire in the Chapel Hill Public Library . . . in a booth at Breadmen's . . . at a picnic table at University Lake . . . on a quilt at Umstead Park . . . in a wicker chair on my own back porch on Burlage Circle. I am writing a novel. I am always writing a novel in this town. Nobody cares. Nobody bugs me. Nobody thinks a thing about it. Everybody else is writing a novel, too.

Doris Betts has said, "In Chapel Hill, throw a rock and you'll hit a writer." This has always been true. For Chapel Hill is primarily a town of the mind, a town of trees and visions. Thomas Wolfe praised the "rare romantic quality of the atmosphere." Maybe the quiet, leafy streets themselves are still informed by his giant spirit, that wild young man from the mountains who raged through them in his archetypal search for identity.

The much-loved English professor Hugh Holman once wrote, "The primary thing that Chapel Hill gives those who come to be a part of it is the freedom to be themselves. It is an unorganized town. It is easy to persuade its citizens, along with the students of the university, to join briefly in a cause, to march for a little while beneath a banner. . . . But to remain permanently organized is something else indeed, for Chapel Hill does not organize very well. Those who come to this town can find in it just about the quantity of freedom to be themselves which they wish to have."

CIRCA 1980

I am with my children, and we run into some of their friends from preschool and the friends' mother.

"Hello, Naomi," I say. "Hi, Johnny."

"We have changed our names," their mother says. "This is Trumpet Vine," she says, indicating Naomi, "and this is Golden Sun. I myself am Flamingo."

Oh my, I think. *Oh no.* My kids do not think that Trumpet Vine is a very good name. But then my younger son, Page, changes his own name (briefly) to Rick. Soon after this, Trumpet Vine, Golden Sun and Flamingo move away from Chapel Hill with some kind of sect.

I never changed my name to Flamingo, but I have thought about it ever since.

SPRING 1983

Now I am divorced. I am walking in the woods with a man, following one of the green-space trails that run all over town, when suddenly we come upon a life-size concrete hippo, climbing out of Bolin Creek as if emerging from the Blue Nile. *Oh no*, I think stupidly, *a hippo!* I take a good look at the man I'm with and realize that we'll probably get married.

JANUARY 1984

A Snapshot of the End of My Youth. Chapel Hill Community Center. A recreation-department basketball game is in progress. My son's team, the Tigers, is ahead by two points, but it's nip and tuck all the way. "Shoot, Monty, shoot!" yells somebody's father, sitting next to me. For some reason, I turn and look at this father. He's an attractive black man wearing a leather hat and a diamond ring. For some reason, he looks familiar. Then it hits me. *Oh no! It's Doug Clark! Of Doug Clark and the Hot Nuts!* He's got a kid, Monty, on the opposing team. . . . *Oh no. I am really old.*

JUNE 29, 1985

Amity, age thirteen and very grown up, has specified a church wedding for her father and me, and so here we are at the Chapel of the Cross, rehearsing hurriedly for our tiny 10 A.M. ceremony, which will take place in less than an hour. Radiant in her white dress, Amity walks endlessly up and down the aisle carrying her bouquet, carrying herself just so. She looks beautiful. But the ladies arranging flowers at the altar scowl at her, whispering among themselves, casting dark looks at the middle-aged groom.

Finally one of the ladies says acidly to me, "Just how old *is* she, anyway?" and I realize that they think *she's* the bride, not me in my green linen dress. *Oh no.* This is what I get for fancying myself a bride at my age! I ought to know better. I ought to stay single and write novels out in the woods.

But then, forty minutes later, I *am* the bride, and I am the happiest bride ever, as the organ plays and the bells ring and we step out into the bright

June day *married*, of all things, and my boys wave at some other boys who are skating on skateboards down Franklin Street.

MAY 1992

My husband and I lean back in porch chairs at our place in the mountains, this faraway place we have wanted for so long, and gaze out on endless clear distance, empty air, then ridge on blue ridge. Ashe County. I remember the old man who told me once, "I need a mountain to rest my eyes against."

I do, too.

This ridge top may be heaven.

Or maybe not.

It's also possible that heaven will turn out to be the Christmas show at the old Rhythm Alley in Chapel Hill, and the Red Clay Ramblers will be playing. Outside it'll be real cold with the promise of snow, but inside it'll be warm and packed with everybody I ever knew, and I'll get a beer and sit down, and the crowd will get quiet, and then Tommy Thompson will pick up his banjo.

Lee Smith is a native of southwest Virginia but a longtime resident Tar Heel who teaches in the graduate writing program at North Carolina State University. She is the author of eleven works of fiction, with a short novel, Christmas Letters, forthcoming.

CLYDE EDGERTON

A Creek Runs through It

My wife, Susan, and I are building a new home in

rural Orange County. A creek, about ten feet wide, runs in front of the site. On the creek bank stands a very large oak tree situated in a bend so that the water heads straight for the tree and has washed dirt away from some of its deep roots. Behind a large exposed root and up under the bank is—was—a small cave. This cave was full of water until I decided to save the tree from eventual toppling.

The decision to save the tree came as a consequence of a need. This tree-saving need arose after I found that a bridge-building need could not be met.

See, it all started when we bought the land, about ten acres, and decided to build a house. (Or rather, hire a builder to do it.) The obvious site was across a creek and at the top of a twenty-foot bluff. Somewhere, a driveway would have to cross the creek.

The obvious crossing was down the creek a short way from the bluff, where the land was level. I decided that my project—a fun project, just enough to engage me without causing great pain, just enough to satisfy my pioneering spirit—would be to build a wooden bridge. Then I could say to my buddies, most of whom built their own houses or at least wired them (the reason I, a non-carpenter and former college professor, have all these carpenter friends is a long story)—anyway, I could say to my buddies, "Naw, I decided not to build the house myself, but I did build that bridge there."

So I was very excited about the prospect of rolling up my sleeves, buying a couple of telephone poles to lay across the creek, some two-by-eights, nails and all that, and get to work. Sweat a little bit. You know. I figured I could hire somebody to "help" me. The secret is: At that point, I was more excited about the bridge than about the house.

By this time, I'd hired an architect. I wanted to do things right. I told the architect, Dail Dixon of Chapel Hill, that I was going to build the bridge. He looked at me funny. Two days later, he called me and said, "We might have a problem with your building that bridge."

"Why?"

"Well, that creek is in a flood plain and—"

"So I'll build a sturdy bridge."

"No. The federal government has structural guidelines—codes—since the bridge is to be in a flood plain, and I'm not sure you can handle what I think they have in mind. You're looking at a rather major construction job. Culverts, riprap and so forth."

"What's riprap?"

"Those big rocks you see around some state bridge constructions and along the banks of some state lakes."

"Oh." The image of a sturdy pioneer-type wooden bridge across the little creek gave way to a picture of I-40 over the Mississippi.

What happened next is an eight-month blur. My able architect started communicating with the appropriate federal agency—FEMA, the Federal Emergency Management Agency. One of its jobs is to protect wetlands by saying what kind of bridge you can build over creeks that are in wetlands.

The way they protect wetlands is this: First, they tell you what kind of bridge you must have. Second, you build it. Third, you never build your house near the wetlands because the bridge costs so much you can't afford to build a house anymore. Thus, people stay away from wetlands and FEMA does its job.

The bridge-approval business took eight months. I'm not talking bridge building, I'm talking bridge approval. The people who planned the bridge to government specifications had to produce two books full of graphs that showed the effects of that one prospective bridge on water flow, water level, etc., in case of flooding. Each book was an inch or so thick. Big books, small print. Many letters were written. Approval was finally granted.

Next: County approval for building the bridge. In order for Orange County to approve—well, let's just stop here on all that and say that the bridge was finally approved by everyone in America over the age of forty-three except the third cousin of a drugstore owner in Ahoskie. And was finally built.

But while the bridge was being approved (and I grew old) and after I realized I'd have no part in planning or building it, I looked for something else I might accomplish.

The tree. Situated on the creek bank at the base of the bluff on which the house would stand, the big beautiful oak seemed in danger of losing its root support and falling because of the force of the running water. The government couldn't stop me from saving the tree, I figured. (Though I didn't run the risk of inquiring.)

My first task, as I saw it, was to do something about the water in the small cavelike hole in the creek bank. The obvious answer was to fill it up with something so that the big hole would not continue to enlarge because of running water. Should I fill it up with riprap? No. Far too commercial. This was pioneer time, frontier time. Should I ask somebody who knew more about this than I did? A tree person, for example? No. All my grandparents were farmers, people of the land. They were independent sorts. So was I. Sort of.

Now, just what would my ancestors do? Why, they'd do what had to be done. They'd use their own rocks, and they'd do all the work themselves.

Up that twenty-foot bluff and beyond the house site were several areas of boulders and smaller rocks. I decided I would somehow use large rocks to fill in under and along the bank at the base of the tree.

I bought a special wheelbarrow with two large bicycle wheels. I loaded it with large rocks—flattening the tires—rolled it to the top of the bluff and threw the rocks, one at a time, down the bluff and into the creek near my needy oak. After three loads (about seven twenty-pound rocks a load), I walked down to the shallow babbling creek, picked up a large rock with both hands and heaved it into the hole under my oak tree. *Ka-splash.* The rock sank out of sight. Rock after rock went into the hole until finally, sometime the next day—after a good night's sleep—the hole was filled. In a week, the cave was full of rocks and the creek bank near my tree was lined with large rocks at water level. My immediate task was complete, I thought.

Then I began to realize that the ground on top of the bank was weak around the tree trunk, regardless of my rock fortress below, and that my only real hope for saving the tree (if indeed it was ever in trouble) would be to divert the stream. I decided I'd better not do that. Then I decided I should. Just dig a trench somehow. Then I decided against that.

My builder, Scott McLean, started building my house on the bluff above the creek, and I lost interest in the tree for about a month, knowing I'd return to my task eventually—before spring rains next year anyway. Then Don Becker, the on-site builder, called and said, "Clyde, you've got a big tree down."

"Oh, no," I said. I pictured my beloved tree lying across the creek, dead. "Is it the big oak at the bottom of the bluff and in the creek bend?"

"I believe it is."

That had to be the one. No other in the area was in danger of falling without reason.

I remembered my days of labor and my warm friendly feelings toward that old oak. That tree and I had a special kind of bond. I had tried in vain to save its life. *Bonanza*. The Cartwrights. Cowboy Country. *Old Yeller*. All that. I felt guilty. If I had only called a tree person instead of going it alone and not really finishing what I'd . . .

I drove out to the creek.

My old oak, lo and behold, was standing as tall as ever. Another tree, of less interest to me, had fallen.

Today I called a tree person, and we have an appointment to meet near the old oak next week. He will tell me what can be done and I will, with renewed vigor, start in on another phase of tree saving.

But something tells me he may look at my handiwork and suggest that I stay out of the woods, except to perhaps bird-watch.

What I've decided to do is this: Trim up to the break point on that big tree that just fell, then lean the ax against it and leave it there. When one of my carpenter buddies notices and says, "What's going on over there?" I'll say, "Oh, just gathering a little firewood." Then he'll say, "You cut that thing down with an ax?"

And I'll say in my deepest frontier voice, "Oh, yeah. Chain saws ain't my style."

Clyde Edgerton's new book is Redeye, *recently out from Penguin. He teaches creative writing at Millsaps College in Jackson, Mississippi. In his spare time, he drives a small bulldozer and watches* Rescue 911 *with his family.*

JILL McCORKLE

. . . .

Native Daughter

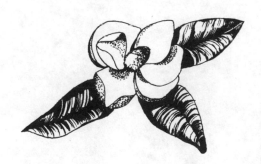

Barely a month into my move to

New England and the question most

often asked is: How long before you start writing about "the North"? I'm usually introduced as someone from "the South," which implies that of course I've spent lengthy time in every Confederate state and am well versed in the history of each. Then it's up to me to erase those pictures of Monticello and Tara, New Orleans and the Everglades, Opryland and Atlanta, and lead them south of Williamsburg and north of "South of the Border," east of Tennessee and west of the Atlantic. I offer mountains, sandhills and the coastal plain, finally settling in the southeastern part of the state in my hometown. I give them miles of flatness, broad sky and open fields, the tea-colored Lumber River winding its way through lush marshland.

As to the question about my writing—well, I find it hard to believe that I will ever, regardless of where I am, feel removed from my origin. We all have that place in memory that stirs emotions, inspires us to do whatever we do. And mine is North Carolina, more specifically Lumberton, still more specifically this region as it was in the sixties and early seventies. That's my fictional source, the backdrop I envision when creating characters and situations, and it's a place and time that offer me a smorgasbord of sensory images, images that never change; without them, I would never have felt the urge to write a word.

This landscape is so entwined with my own life and the way I view the world that it appears naturally. Once I thought I was writing a piece that was without strong Southern influence, only to complete the novel and find that I had someone who was forced to attend a C of C (Children of the Confederacy) meeting, and I had a statue in the center of town erected to the memory of the Confederate dead. I had pines and magnolias and iced tea at every turn.

I realized then that there was no way around it. My characters go to Raleigh for shopping and culture. They take their medical problems to Duke and N.C. Memorial. They get their furniture in High Point, and they fly out of RDU. They go to N.C. State, Coastal Community College. They go on dates to South of the Border, get married in Dillon and make it back over the state line before the eleven o'clock news.

My scenes are annual ones, my characters driven and controlled by the seasons and weather. In the fall, they go out and pick up pecans, shell and store them for the holiday baking. They find all kinds of interesting ways to decorate with pine cones. On some clear Saturday morning, they drive northward to Chapel Hill, where they pile into Kenan Stadium, sing "Hark, the Sound of Tar Heel Voices" and wave blue-and-white pompons that match the sky; they stop by the Old Well to pose for photos and go to the Carolina Coffee Shop (or K & W) for supper.

These people have freak snowfalls that absolutely paralyze the town, and kids dash off with cookie sheets and pasteboard boxes to the overpass hills of the interstate to sled. They have brief springs, a burst of dogwoods and aza-leas. High-school kids drive thirty minutes toward the coast to collect Span-ish moss that they drape—along with old parachutes—over the bleachers in the gymnasium. They turn out in rented tuxes and frilly prom dresses to dance to Harley Hogg and the Rockers from Lizard Lick. They step outside for a breath of cool air, but already it feels like summer.

Ah, those North Carolina summers. This is the season that seems to greet my characters more than any other. Their legs stick to hot vinyl car seats. They squint and shield their eyes; makeup runs and hairstyles droop. There is the constant rumble and drone of air conditioners and window fans. There's the smell of cut grass and watermelon and chlorine from the local pool where children stay from morning to night.

And of course, there's the summer vacation when they drive that short dis-tance to the North Carolina coast (my characters tend to visit Long and Holden Beaches), and they fish off the weathered piers, the salty air smelling of cut bait and Coppertone. They plan their days around the tides, finding buckets of sand dollars and conch shells. Kids body-surf and play Putt-Putt; they walk down to the inlet with a bucket of fish heads for crabbing. The teen-agers drive over to Myrtle to ride the Swamp Fox and then go to O.D. to shag at the Spanish Galleon. At night, the whole family drives to Calabash for sup-per, and then they venture out with sweaters over sunburned skin, and they twirl sparklers and watch the beacon of the Fort Caswell lighthouse.

In late summer and early fall, their town is bathed in the sweet heavy scent of tobacco. Large trucks rumble through the downtown streets as they carry the loads to the warehouses. Young boys work there, summer after summer, learning about the market. They walk home sweaty-dirty with the rich smell in their hair and clothes. When they ride by the big warehouses, the alumi-num doors are often swung open, and the line of buyers moves like a snake through the bundles of leaves. The auctioneer's voice, a quick cadence of numbers, rises and falls on the air stirred by the huge fans up above. Children collect the loose leaves that fall from the trucks and use them for an Indian headdress, or a talisman, or they sneak off to a neighborhood tree house to crumble a bit of the golden leaf and roll it into a tiny piece of paper, light it with a match.

Sometimes, out of moral or medical or enlightened reasoning, I try to curb my characters, but try as I might, one will inevitably light up, or one will spend his summer vacation working in the market, or one will step out onto the porch and breathe in that distinct smell that even in memory brings a flood of associations.

My characters tend vegetable gardens, bitter-smelling tomatoes and thick rows of corn, the silks ranging from white to pink to a dark tangled brown, which children use to fashion hair for people they draw in the dirt. While grownups dig potatoes, the children are digging for colored glass and marbles, their pockets filled with the treasures they deposit in garages and toolsheds, dirt-floored structures, damp and dark, the light from the door falling in a wide slant onto shelves of canned peaches and tomatoes, jewel tones similar to the metallic-tasting aluminum tumblers that are in their grandmothers' kitchen cabinets.

My characters experience the building of interstates. They live in neighborhoods where children stay out until the streetlights come on. A train passes and all the kids collect to place pennies on the tracks and to wave to the old rough-looking, tobacco-chewing man standing at the rail of the caboose. (He becomes their sinister image, the face for the old man close by who is rumored to shoot children who run through the garden.) They spend hours climbing the clay walls of a drainage ditch, pressing their cheeks to the damp yellow-and-red earth as they sniff for sassafras roots.

In the land on the other side, there are woods and a field full of grassy weeds. There is a loose wild chicken and the threat of snakes; but there are also plump juicy blackberries everywhere. And just beyond the woods, there are bulldozers and big trucks, the smell of pitch mixing with tobacco as the interstate plows through, bringing with it Howard Johnson and Holiday Inn, Pizza Hut and McDonald's.

They ride bikes on the service road and marvel at the funny accents of people who stop at the Texaco station on the corner. They sit way up under the concrete overhangs of the overpass where it's cool and count license plates. For my characters, the interstate represents progression; it gives them an exit, a road to schools and malls and beaches and other states, and it gives them an easy way home.

To make a very long, meandering story short, North Carolina remains the solid base for everything that goes into my work. There is nothing I can totally separate from my life and history there. Oh, there may be an occasional character who grew up in a different place, but that character is the exception to the rule, not to mention that that character is usually in a Southern setting, hearing very distinct North Carolina accents.

My four-year-old daughter recently drew and colored a blue circle (the world) and then set about filling in the brown dots of land. She asked me to write the names of these places as she dictated, and we wound up with Lumberton, Durham, Chapel Hill, New York (my husband's home state), Boston, London and the beach. By my estimation, North Carolina makes up 50 percent of the world. I realize that my own childhood vision (North Carolina, Lumberton and Texas) gave the state a slightly higher percentage, but I do have to take into account that both my parents were natives and that I spent my entire childhood there. As for my fictional world, I give North Carolina a percentage of 99; it will always be my strongest point of memory, a source as constant as the Lumber River.

And as different as Boston may be—weather and accent and foliage and history—I take great comfort in the fact that the Atlantic Ocean is within easy reach and that just a few miles from this very spot is I-95, reminding me with glittering asphalt and huge green signs that I can turn right, head south and in about fifteen hours cross the state line. One thing I know is that I can always go back. It will be a cold July in Robeson County—a fall without football (the ACC without basketball!)—it will be a world without interstates, before I ever give up the roots.

*A native North Carolinian, **Jill McCorkle** is the author of four novels and a book of short stories. Her new novel, Carolina Moon, will be published in the fall of 1996. She teaches creative writing at Harvard University and spends much of her time shoveling snow.*

WILLIAM McCRANOR HENDERSON

The Return of the Native

"Actually . . . I grew up in Chapel Hill."

It's uncanny, the effect of those words in conversation. People take a step back and blink at me, as if I had just said, "You know, I have an extra ear." We are a rare breed— like native Californians in West L.A. or born-and-bred New Yorkers in Manhattan. And with Chapel Hill itself so much a city of the recently arrived, it's inevitable that those few of us who started off here should be virtually invisible.

I can understand it better, I think, because my own status is paradoxical: Even though I spent both childhood and youth here, I too am a recent arrival, a returnee— a prodigal son. My experience with something called "the Triangle," for instance, is only three years old. There was no Triangle when I was a kid. There was Raleigh (a hellish drive along Old 54); there was

Durham, not today's "City of Medicine," but a younger, brighter, more allit-erative "City of Exciting Stores." In between, it was all farm and forest.

There were no malls. On downtown Franklin Street, you could buy pretty much whatever you needed (at full-service emporiums like Belk, Berman's, Huggins', etc.); or if your needs were special, there was always Durham's glitter-ing, sophisticated "Five Points," and one of the aforementioned "exciting stores."

There were no suburbs, no schools scattered through the county woods. I went through twelve years of public school entirely inside the downtown rect-angle that today encloses University Square and the Granville Towers com-plex. And with all my schooling centered downtown—with *everything* centered downtown—you can bet that a good chunk of my youth was spent on the UNC campus.

It wouldn't be inaccurate to call me and my cronies, from age ten, say, through junior high, "recreationally deprived." We had to create our own hangouts. (Example: Sloan Drugs, on the corner where Spanky's now sits, was a key haunt.) The campus was smaller and sleepier in those days and was managed in an amiably lackadaisical fashion. Hence, we used UNC for our own purposes: The campus itself became our unofficial youth center, our coun-try club. We were "campus rats."

As kids, we knew the best places to jump a bike, the best trees to climb in, the drink machines you could jimmy for a free Pepsi. For a pack of ten-year-olds with two-wheelers, the campus teemed with potential, a living game board of secrets, thrills, opportunities.

Later on, as jaded teenagers, we would dress cool and strut like college sophs, slip into fraternity rush bashes, play pickup basketball in Woollen Gym, get into fierce gang snowball fights with the SAEs, Dekes, ATOs as we swept through town with nothing else to do on declared snow days (yes, it snowed in those days!).

But as I look back, one year, and one set of memories, stands out gilt-edged, photo-vivid, as sharp and permanent as memory can get. It is the year 1957—the academic year '56–'57, to be exact—the year Tar Heel basketball first thrust

Chapel Hill into the glare of national media prominence.

It wasn't just that I was such a basketball fan (although I was), it wasn't just the offbeat quality of the team itself—an Irish coach from New York City, playing four Irish guys and a Jew (the great Lennie Rosenbluth), all from "up there." It's not even that this crazy team went undefeated all the way to the NCAA championship. What stands out in my memory is how, that season, as a thirteen-year-old half-boy, half-man, I used my considerable campus-rat skills to (forgive me, Lord) gate-crash every home game.

It was simple. In those days, Carolina's home court was tiny Woollen Gym, with its minuscule seating capacity of five thousand. Fans perched in rickety wooden bleachers and screamed with end-of-the-world intensity. Close quarters had the effect of creating a kind of hysteria I've never witnessed in the "wine-and-cheese" atmosphere of the vast, airy Dean Dome. Seating was a jam-them-in kind of affair. There were seat numbers, but they were impossible to read. No one paid much attention to them anyway since, instead of individual chair backs, your reserved seat was simply a space along a bare board. Once you were inside, with or without a ticket, you could squeeze in just about anywhere, blending into the mass of seating along any given row.

On game days, we would play pickup ball in Woollen until late afternoon, when they cleared the gym to prepare for the evening event. But instead of leaving, we would file surreptitiously into the spacious corner men's room, lock ourselves into stalls, and sit patiently, waiting for six o'clock. By then, the "ticket gates" (mere long tables) would have been set up out in the main lobby, the freshman preliminary game would be under way (freshmen had their own team back then), and by mere virtue of being inside the men's room, we were, ipso facto, "in." At a given signal (a single flush by whoever had a watch), we filed out and merged into the entering crowd stream, picking our spots along choice bleacher rows and squeezing politely left or right if challenged by a real ticket holder.

Those who lived through that season will probably remember it as producing more "great" games—cliffhangers, blood-and-guts overtime battles decided by last-minute heroics—than any other single Carolina basketball season. That at least is the way I recall it, in large-scale cinematic memories that reflect my physical vantage point, usually mere yards away from the action—the kind of seat Jack Nicholson gets at the Forum in L.A. What we did was outrageous. But those were simpler days. My buddies and I were the village wise guys: Old enough to know how to manipulate a simple, trusting system, young enough not to be ashamed of ourselves for violating UNC's serendipitous institutional naiveté.

Things aren't like that anymore. Today, as far as I know, no one—certainly not a bunch of scraggly local preteens—sneaks into the Dean Dome. And if they do, there are now legions of tough, middle-aged "ushers" to escort them ignobly back into the night. The only sports practice I've carried over from my campus-rat days involves buying tickets: I never go to the box office; I snag better seats five minutes before game time, from the hawkers outside. The same goes for football at Kenan Stadium, where, as a slightly older campus rat, I myself was once one of those hawkers, buying low and selling high, and did pretty well at it.

Today, though I've proved to myself that you can go home again, it still takes some getting used to. At times, when I trot out my stories of the old Chapel Hill, I feel like (apologies to Allan Gurganus) the Oldest Living Confederate Survivor Telling All. *Listen: There was this sleazy, highly anarchistic old beer joint, "The Shack," right next to the old town hall—which is now the homeless shelter. . . . Right beside it was the falling-down chicken-wire-lined shed where I would pick up a bundle of Durham Suns for my afternoon paper route. . . . We'd play cowboys behind the stores on Franklin Street, where there were secluded old homes with carefully tended gardens and serpentine walks, some lived in by old ladies struggling at the edges of respectability, some taken over by beatnik roomers. . . . And hear this: No one in town was rich like today's Triangle Park CEOs with their enormous new suburban palaces. At the top of the tree were a few doctors and professors, and they seemed to live in comparatively modest splendor on Gimghoul Road or Tenney Circle. . . . Listen: Nothing "big" ever happened here. The world only visited Chapel Hill on certain football Saturdays. . . . People came to Chapel Hill to get away from the world.*

Now the world has come to Chapel Hill—some people's worst nightmare. But quite frankly, with all the moaning about the demise of "the Southern Part of Heaven," this new sophistication, this new richness, is one of the reasons I'm back. As a writer, I never wrote "Southern," and there is a simple reason for this: I'm a Southerner who has spent his entire adult life living in the North. This was by choice. As often as I experienced ridicule, misunderstanding, condescension among the heathen, I wouldn't have had things any other way. I grew up wanting to be where the books I read were published, where the Broadway plays I loved were staged, where the TV I watched was made, where cat-slick men and women dwelled in apartments with views of the Manhattan skyline and drank martinis in the morning. I was a provincial yearning for the center. I ran from the South just as I would have run from the farms of Minnesota, the backwoods of Maine, the plains of Texas.

In Northerners, I admired a certain peppy energy and enterprise that were too often passed off in the South as mere vulgarity. The Midwestern-born narrator in a story of mine says, "In all the movies I saw as a kid growing up back there in Nowheresville, the characters who appealed to me were the wise guys, the clever ones, the operators—Jews, Italians, Irish city slickers, fast on the take, never stuck for a line, always on their way up" (just the kinds of characters, it seemed to me, that had lit up Woollen Gym back in '57). As a kid, I longed for Chapel Hill to be cross-pollinated with a non-Southern strain of attitude and behavior, but since it wasn't happening fast enough for me, I was out of here.

Now it has happened, for better and for worse. My children are growing up here without Southern accents (I wish there were something I could do to change that!), but I suppose the message has to be: Don't ask too much. I like what I see in Chapel Hill now. The one-time village is growing gawkily into its citified maturity—with new, urban-style kinds of problems, to be sure; and yes, full of fast-talking Yankees who don't even feel pressured to say "y'all" every now and then and who gape with wonder at an authentic Chapel Hill–bred middle-aged adult. But it's certainly a more profuse environment, full of all those resources you once had to leave the area for. Some die-hard local friends of mine claim that what they see is no less than the end of civilization as they knew it—as we all once knew it. This is undeniable. But as for me, re-ensconced in my childhood house and haunting UNC three days a week as a legitimate employee, I'm having too much fun finding new places to jump my bike to pay the apocalypse much mind.

William McCranor Henderson is a native North Carolinian who never wore the tar off his heels no matter how far he roamed. After a twenty-five-year hiatus, he returned to Chapel Hill in 1989 and has since taught fiction writing at the University of North Carolina and North Carolina State University. He writes books, and lives in the house he grew up in, with wife Carol and daughters Olivia and Colette.

ELIZABETH SPENCER

Heading for the Hills

When I was growing up, a barefoot

kid in the benighted Mississippi of the

Depression years, North Carolina was just about the only state I knew about. "You didn't know about Mississippi?" Understand that Mississippi, if you grow up there, is not really a state—it is a country, the world, the human condition, the universe. Or was in the years I speak of. I was aware of a state called New Hampshire because an uncle had a summer house there on the shores of a strangely named lake that sounded like something out of *The Song of Hiawatha* and of Wisconsin because another uncle had gone north to make a better living and got married there. But North Carolina was first and foremost what was meant by another place than home for various reasons, here to be told.

The mountains were there. These were pre–air conditioning days. In summer, Mississippi heat was so hellishly oppressive, so constant and debilitating that anyone who could afford the trip escaped to wherever possible. My mother suffered, or so she professed, more than anyone else from the interminable succession of baking hundred-degree days and stifling ninety-degree nights. She hoped and prayed for the good cotton crop that would get her to the North Carolina mountains.

Montreat was her heart's goal. Her entire family had always been Presbyterian, and the "seat" for the Southern branch of the faith was there. The General Assembly was held there, and there the finest of the clergy were known to preach. But more sacred than all these, it was cool! Cool nights! Chill rushing streams murmured through the peaceful hours, and rhododendron blossoms hung dewy above, no wilting heat to shrivel them. Clouds sat on the mountaintops or, drifting lower, curled along winding roads and pathways, pleasantly moist to the flesh. "Think how hot it is back home!" she would exclaim, as if anything was needed to add to the delight of that marvelous escape.

I myself remember that I did not so much mind the summer weather. Ladies went about in stockings and petticoats and wore gloves and hats, and the painted fans they were always unfurling to war against the heat of the gigantic oven we lived and breathed in did little except tire them out while stirring up the air. Inside, electric fans buzzed constantly; neither parlors nor offices were complete without at least one, hard at work. Iced tea and lemonade layered pitchers with sweat as thick as rain.

I went around barefoot in shorts and a minuscule top. There was a swimming place to go to in the afternoon, and later on, when the shadows got longer, everyone gathered at the tennis court out to the side of our property. Cold watermelon, fetched from the town icehouse, greeted the conclusion of our matches.

But back in the spring one year, I had heard some ominous talk going around—I was not as healthy as I should be; maybe I should be sent to camp.

Camp. Gradually, I began to consider this unusual notion. Maybe it wouldn't be so bad, even interesting maybe. I wrote off for catalogs. There was Camp

Lake Junaluska, for instance, attractive, but it was Methodist, and there was no use, I must have seen early on, getting hooked on anything Baptist or Episcopalian either—much less purely a camp, run as a business with no religion in mind. (Maybe they thought I needed more religion? I forget, now, if this aspect was mentioned.) Camp Montreat, it should have been clear from the first moment, was to be the choice.

Away from home and into the mountains. We met a group at a nearby railroad station; a counselor was there to attend to us. Our bags contained all items we were advised to bring. The lists had been checked, the name tapes dutifully sewed on. White slacks for outings, shorts and shirts for every day, bathing suit and beach towel, hiking shoes and tennis shoes, white dress for church—what a lot of care goes into these plannings for first departures from home! On the train, the talk was lively among those who knew each other from past years, but I was no part of that and scarcely knew what to say to them. I must have got homesick before we crossed the state line into Tennessee.

But when morning came after a night in a Pullman berth, what did I see out the window but the Earth, turned green as springtime, tilted vertically up, right into the sky itself, no top in sight. We were in the mountains.

At camp itself, I was miserable. We learned a lot of songs, and it rained a lot. We had scheduled tennis and scheduled crafts, archery, riding and, worst of all, swimming. I loved swimming as a general rule, but the water in an awful pond named Lake Susan was so cold it made your teeth chatter to approach it. There we went, I can see as if from above, a wavering little file on bare spindly legs, large beach towels hugged about our thin shoulders, with bathing caps and rubber sandals, trudging down a rocky path toward thirty minutes of sheer freezing torture. The swimming instructor, flat chested and butch, with a boy's name and close-cropped hair, stood on the bank and put us through it—sidestroke and breaststroke and crawl. We finished with a free-for-all race and came out blue and quavering to climb the path, free for another day.

Then there was the mountain climbing. An awful toil it was. We started with a mountain called Greybeard for some reason of configuration. The ascent was supposed to be easy—the son of the camp director would go and run up it after supper to see the sun set—but the twisting slippery paths held little charm for me. The gullies and eroded hills of Carroll County back home had been good enough. On top of the mountain, we saw the views and sang the songs and ate the picnic. Then we came down. I used to spend time studying the calendar. The camp session lasted two months. The weeks were slow.

The ones in my age group and myself slept in a huge second-story room of one of the central camp buildings. There were ten or more double-decker bunk beds lined against three of the four walls. We kept our clothes and small effects in suitcases shoved beneath the beds or hung on pegs along the walls. There was one bathroom. I had drawn a lower berth. Directly next to me, on the upper bunk, was a girl named Lillian, though called "Shanghai." She was from the North Carolina coast. During rest period, which lasted every day for an hour after lunch, she used to lean over the edge of the bunk and describe her life at the seacoast to me in whispers. She lived alone with her father, she said. He worked, and she would go down to the beach and walk along until she met some boy. He would say, "Hi, Shanghai, where you going?" She would say, "Nowhere particularly," and they would hang around together. This was how her days passed. I began to want to go to the Carolina coast myself. I can see now why her father must have thought it a good idea to send her off to camp.

Often, at night, the camp director, a really pretty widow, would come up and talk to us about her religious beliefs, speaking with utter sincerity and simplicity. She always prayed for us aloud before we loaded up in the truck bed and went caroling away on one of our Saturday trips to the Biltmore Estate or some other place too distant for hiking to. She would read a Psalm about the Lord preserving our going out and our coming in for now and evermore. It is easy to see that she lived with the worry that someone might fall off a mountain or get snakebit. A tragic accident was about all that was needed to upset her precarious financial balance. She could often be observed in her rooms with her bright head of hair bent down over account books. At any rate, the Lord heeded her: we all lived.

In the middle of this sojourn, so kindly conceived of as the place I was to improve in health, meet new people, gain weight, have fun, a letter arrived announcing that my mother, brother and two aunts were on the way. A terrible pretender, I had written glowing letters home about how wonderful everything was, but another, truer message had somehow got through between the lines of these awkwardly written missives. I was thought to be homesick. The idea! I replied. Nevertheless, when, a week later, the family car pulled up the twisting road from the lake, I felt the key strike the prison door. No more ice water or wearisome clambering over slimy moss. No more shouting songs with silly words. No more scheduled play. Liberation was at hand.

It may be that my mother and aunts had invented the whole plan of my rescue from homesickness in order to get to North Carolina. At any rate, I joined the party, and the mountains took on another aspect entirely, as the view was now something not demanding to be hiked through. My mother and aunts would never have dreamed of climbing anything beyond steps with balustrades, and my brother never mentioned it either. We were tourists in a beautiful land, which I could see for the first time without thinking how not to cry. Little Switzerland was a day trip, and Chimney Rock another; the camera was often out. The mountain air they delighted in became wonderfully breathable to me as well, "pure ozone," they called it, and we followed twisting roads both up and down, dizzy with daring and danger, hoping the car would make it and the radiator would not explode.

These then, that summer, were the Smokies, my first mountains. I came back to say good-bye to my friends at camp and be present at the closing night banquet where many tears flowed freely from those parting with such dearly loved friends. I wonder how much of this outpouring was not simply the adolescent need to have as many emotions as possible. I loved everybody there the minute I didn't have to see them any longer.

Finally, we arrived back home, descending by degrees into the Deep South with its long baked stretches of road, its wide fields, its summer-weary towns. When we drove into our own property, I was most astonished by the trees.

They looked taller than when I had left—the oaks, the pecans, the walnut and crape myrtles—and the leaves seemed to have shrunk under the constant battering of heat so that sunlight rained slanting through them, splashing down in spatters of light on the dry soil.

A later season had come in my absence. Soon, there would be school once more.

It was the mountains that lingered with me. Their lofty outline against evening skies, the rosy corona the sunset left as it faded, seemed when I withdrew from it irreplaceable. Surprising myself, I longed to return, to have it back once more. For both air and atmosphere are singularly different up there in that region around Asheville. And Asheville itself grew importantly larger for me as I read more and found one afternoon, absorbed beneath the trees in the front yard in Mississippi, how a young man named Thomas Wolfe had grown up there, lived along its streets, known its people and climbed into the sunlit mountain stillness hand in hand with his first love.

According to **Elizabeth Spencer**, *her native Mississippi is "said to be illiterate as well as barefoot, but mysteriously good at literature." Since her first novel was published in 1948, she has "gone scooting around the world from home base' in the South, to Italy, to Canada, and now back to North Carolina." She is the author of nine novels and four short-story collections.*

MAX STEELE

. . . .

The House of Their Childhood

For a while we had a house in Beaufort looking

out across Taylors Creek at Bird Shoals and the inlet to the Atlantic Ocean. From the porch or through the downstairs windows we could see our lawn, full of sandburrs, the street, our boathouse and dock, the creek and beyond it the dunes where the wild horses came during storms, the young colts in their midst.

From the upstairs windows we could see the entire island, a part of the Outer Banks, all the way from the town harbor to Shackleford Banks. The little island is maybe three miles long and over a half-mile wide at high tide. At low tide there is a mud flat that cuts deep between the dunes and the wide ocean-side beach. At high tide the mud flat is flooded by ocean water up to a tall man's knees.

The North Carolina coast at this point runs strangely east and west and so from our porch we looked south toward Panama, Ecuador and Lima, Peru, and not, as one might expect, toward Morocco, Algiers and Cairo, Egypt. But truth to tell, when the children were small we thought almost not at all of distant lands, we were so busy exploring our own private sand bar.

How did I happen to have a house on the North Carolina coast? I had in 1972 been voted a teaching award by my students and colleagues. Other professors who had won the award in previous years had used the money to pay grocery bills at Fowler's or had bought stereo systems. One man had even taken his wife to breakfast and a weekend in Paris.

What had brought me to Beaufort to buy a house? I had recently been pressed into teaching a course in children's literature in which I required a childhood diary. Much to my surprise I had learned from these diaries that the students who had had vacation homes had the most vivid memories and the happiest ones. So I decided that instead of buying a decent car I would use the money as a down payment on a vacation house. During a long weekend I had gone down the North Carolina coast from Virginia to South Carolina before discovering in Beaufort, on a later trip, an unpainted shack, built by fishermen, that had survived all hurricanes for a hundred years. That first September we had time only to secure it against the winter storms by replacing the linoleum windows with glass panes and to put a new tin roof over the side porch. The first fall and winter I would go down to try to get a bathtub installed (during its hundred years the house had never had one), and a lavatory. And to rig up some sort of heating system.

Late in April I went alone and as I turned down Live Oaks, there across "the Cut," as the natives call the dredged canal which is Taylors Creek, on a low dune an elephant was silhouetted against the evening sky. Near it was a canopy and under the canopy a band of musicians, hippies of the era, playing and singing their hearts out. At first I thought it had happened what I knew would someday happen from reading too many student manuscripts: either I had lost my mind, or Fellini was filming here.

At such times one needs reassurance. I stopped my car and asked the only man walking. He answered quite calmly, hardly breaking his stride: "It's the hippies. They're celebrating the elephant." Had he meant *serenading?*

"An elephant?" I asked because I still did not trust my eyes or his words.

"The carnival man." He paused to look back. "Every year or so he brings the elephant to bathe in the salt water."

That night a huge beach fire lit up the swaying elephant and the dancing hippies. The music got into my dreams and when I would wake I wished I were young and had a boat so that I could row across to be sure where dream ended and land began.

In late May I began bringing my sons, aged three and six, with me to search for a safe boat. The old men who gathered near our boathouse each evening found us a heavy wooden one and were proud when we bought it and not a speedboat as many of the new people were doing.

That summer we begin our ritual of rowing over to the island with our necessities: life preservers, tennis shoes to walk across the mud flat, towels, headgear, lunch and leaf bags. The tide is coming in and we wade across the mud flat and over the warm sand to the beach which stretches a hundred or more yards to the inlet and the ocean. There my wife and I lie on towels while the children search the tide pools for minnows. They see the shadows clearly but not the silvery fish and it is the shadows they try to cup in their hands. To cool we rise and take the children out to the water which slopes out so gently they cannot easily find a place where it is over their heads. Gradually they are swimming and no one knows when they learned. We swim too but mainly we lie on our backs in the shallow water and talk: about sea things, shore things, land things, about our house in Chapel Hill which seems so far away and in the children's memory seems to consist only of their bunk beds and the granite whale rock with the sand pile around it.

But now we are all hungry. Suddenly starving. We open the cooler and take out carrots, cucumbers, cherry tomatoes, homemade bread and hard-boiled eggs. Like raccoons the children wash the vegetables and eggs in seawater to flavor them with just the salty taste of their own remembered tears. We have ice water to drink and now a long nap, covered with towels from the late-morning sun. The walk back seems forever to the boys, who want to be carried. But we each have the leaf bags to tote, filled with other people's litter which apparently washes in from the inlet for we have never yet seen in the daytime any other human beings on the vast expanses of sand and grass. The mud flat now is deep enough with ocean water that the children demand and get a ride on our shoulders. Put down on the other side they race up the sand dune by the Cut that protects the horses during storms. (The horses are not wild after all but belong, we hear, to a doctor who has rigged up a bathtub on the east end which he keeps filled with city water from a garden hose that runs from his yard across the bottom of the forty-foot-deep Cut. True Outer Banks ponies know where to paw holes in the sand and find fresh water to drink.)

In a later summer they have, Diana, Oliver and Kevin, run from the beach across the mud flat (for the boys are old enough now to throw and catch the red Frisbee as they run), the three of them black against the sky in the noon sun. My shadow stays beneath my feet and when I look up I see them on the dune and beyond them our newly stained house with its huge new windows. Now time stands still as it does in rare moments and I know in that still moment that I am as happy as any man alive on this earth. Recently I have had to try to explain to a writing seminar what Joyce meant when he talked about "Epiphany" and I have fumbled around and suggested that he meant that time when a character, in one moment, sees his life against his own destiny and knows something of its meaning.

I call to them to wait for me. "Diana. Oliver. Kevin." Even their names sound beautiful, blown away by the strong ocean wind. I try their longer names and they too sound beautiful yet unheard by all but me. Now here, in the center of the island, in the center of the day, perhaps in the center of my life span, I see my younger son turn back and I hear him call in concern for my safety: "Daddy." The name is still new enough to me to sound tender and I feel its weight in my chest. I am defined. My life is defined by that one word.

I drag the plastic bags full of debris up the sand dune, across the shore of the canal and into the boat. The three of them are swimming on ahead, being carried down toward the menhaden factory and the German veneer factory by the incoming tide.

It is another summer and the boys are now ten and seven. The three of us are exploring the town end of the island where there are trees and a tree house built by Boy Scouts and used by overnighters. (Still we have never met any-one on the beaches, even on the Fourth of July when cars are backed up six blocks waiting to get across the bridge from Morehead City to Atlantic Beach and Fort Macon.) A mare has kicked at Kevin who only wanted to pet her colt so we have come down to the canal with its narrow coast. Suddenly the sand is soft under my feet and suddenly it is up around my knees and waist and I know I am in trouble. As I sink I yell to the boys to go up on the dune. They hear the alarm in my voice and do as I say and I am thinking, how will they get home without me? In my panic I see them younger, unable to swim, unable to row a boat. How will they survive without me? I know that in quick-sand one should throw oneself on one's back but my heart is pounding and my head too. As a child I had asthma and the fear of suffocating overwhelms me. Yet I cannot throw myself on my back. I do not trust such knowledge. I throw myself forward and it works. I am no longer sinking and I do a quick dog paddle for probably not more than a yard or so. I grab a root and then a rock and am out of danger and laughing so that they will not see my panic. I pull myself out of the bottomless sand. My sneakers are gone but I am alive and breathing in gasps. I warn them of such sand and danger and then to wash the fear from their eyes I make light of the misadventure.

Thus the summers go. Now they bring down friends. Now we come and go in different groupings. In two cars and three. There are many guests from around the country, and a plank table on which sits a silver punch bowl full of ice and shrimp and lemon slices. (We have a contract to buy, each year, the first hundred pounds of shrimp from the former owner of the boathouse who still uses it for his nighttime fishing and shrimping.) Parties. More parties. Now there are more things to do at home in Chapel Hill. Now the beach house often stands vacant in the summer or is rented. More parties. At one house or the other. Endless parties. We are no longer there as family. Excitement seems always to be at the house where we are not. And for me there is always a great deal of work to do to keep the place in shape.

Late one October I am there alone as is often the case these days and before I go to bed I look out across Bird Shoals at the moon and at the clouds towering white in the moonlight. The egrets look like white holes in the live oaks. Once golden pheasants nested here in large numbers but the horses have ruined their nesting sites. The horses are along the ridge of a distant dune and the night air smells of salt water and horse dung. Sleep seems far away and I sit on the floor, my arms on the window sill, and listen and wonder if I would trade the braying of the horses for the whirring of golden pheasants.

It is early dawn when I wake, knowing there is some reason I have waked suddenly, but for what reason? Bidden by a silent voice I go to the window. Surely there is a reason: and there it is. Sailing down the Cut toward the harbor is a thirty-foot yacht with three white sails and a few running lights and a light in the cabin. Ahead of it three dolphins are leading the way down to the harbor, leaping, one at a time, all together, one, another, "ten to every fin," the natives say. The silver dolphins play and cavort ahead of the silent boat in the slight mist. I long to follow down to the harbor and out to the inlet, into the open ocean.

And I think in that serene moment, whatever else, let it be said that for a while he had a house that looked out across Bird Shoals to the inlet, and the sea.

Max Steele, *for twenty-one years director of creative writing at the University of North Carolina, is these days seldom seen in Chapel Hill, where he lives a hermitlike existence 335 days a year. But he spends huge amounts of time on the World Wide Web keeping in touch with his sons, grandson, friends and former students. His short-story collection* The Hat of My Mother *was recently reissued by Algonquin Books of Chapel Hill.*

JERRY BLEDSOE
....

Slaw Crazy

Only twice have I been away from North Caro-

lina for extended periods —nearly three years in the army and another six months when I took a job in Kentucky—and both times homesickness kept my belly in almost constant turmoil.

I should not have been surprised that this was the part of my anatomy most directly affected by my longings, I suppose, for a great part of my homesickness had to do with food.

Food, I think, is a major part of anybody's memories of home, and although you might not suspect it to look at my scrawny frame, I am food haunted (skinny people are more obsessed with food than heftier folks, I'm convinced, because we are keenly aware that we are without built-in reserves and know we can't last long without regular replenishment).

I realize that some might argue that there is little about North Carolina cuisine to be missed for very long, or indeed that there is

63

a North Carolina cuisine at all, but I beg to differ. True, North Carolina's traditional cuisine may not be as distinctive and varied as, say, Louisiana's, or New Mexico's, or even that of our more aristocratic neighbors to the north and south, what with Virginia's Colonial fare and South Carolina's Low Country offerings. Still, we have dishes and touches that simply are not to be found elsewhere, and I have discovered that I cannot go long without them.

When I was growing up in Thomasville, most of the meals to which I sat, like those of most other North Carolinians, would have been lumped (and that is an apt description, believe me) under the classification of "country cooking." This was a plain and practical school of cooking that leaned toward fried meats and overboiled vegetables seasoned heavily with pork fat. I don't mean to disparage this type of food, for I frequently crave it still. Neither do I mean to imply that there was anything particularly North Carolinian about it. It was common throughout the South. But despite this, we managed to develop some distinctive and, some might say, peculiar fare of our own, and at the heart of it all, I submit, is a single, simple salad.

Slaw.

Yes, slaw. I don't mean "cole slaw" either. I never heard that term until I was grown and had begun to wander beyond North Carolina's borders, and most of what I saw served under that moniker bore little resemblance to anything I had known before. For several years after I first heard people using it, I thought they were saying "cold slaw" and wondered why they insisted on being redundant. Who would want hot slaw? And wouldn't that make it something else entirely?

No, in North Carolina, it was just *slaw*: finely chopped cabbage with vinegar, sugar, and mayonnaise (although there are a couple of important variations that I will get to momentarily).

I have a friend in Georgia, a cabbage hater of some renown, who insists that North Carolinians are "slaw crazy." We gob slaw on everything we eat, he maintains, and he considers this an affront to civilized behavior second only to our production of tobacco products.

While he is, of course, exaggerating, I must acknowledge that we put slaw to more imaginative uses than most people.

Before the coming of corporate fast food, with its standardized and sterile offerings, North Carolina was the only place on earth where if you asked for a hot dog in a restaurant, it routinely came with mustard, chili, and slaw. Same for hamburgers. I thought that was the only way hot dogs were served until I was sixteen and went with my family to visit distant relatives in upstate New York, where hot dogs, for some quirky reason, were called "red hots." At an amusement park, I ordered a hot dog "all the way," meaning that I wanted onions included with the mustard, chili, and slaw. I was startled when I was handed a concoction with pickle relish, cold sauerkraut, and a smear of brownish goop that bore little resemblance to the bright yellow French's mustard to which I was accustomed, the only mustard I had ever known. Not that I was averse to kraut, mind you. We regularly ate kraut with sliced frankfurters at home, but they were fried together in fatback grease and served with cornbread and pinto beans. "Kraut and wienies," we called that dish, and I eat it still.

I've never been able to pinpoint exactly why or when North Carolinians started putting slaw on hot dogs, hamburgers, and other sandwiches (even the famous porkchop sandwich at Andy and Barney's beloved Snappy Lunch in Mount Airy comes with slaw), but I suspect it has something to do with North Carolina's most distinguished contribution to the culinary arts.

I speak, of course, of barbecue.

Other places have "barbecue" and boast bombastically about it, but nobody understands barbecue better than North Carolinians. Consequently, North Carolina barbecue is unique, superior to all other so-called barbecues on the planet, and without question our state dish, the centerpiece of North Carolina cuisine.

The first thing that North Carolinians understand about barbecue is that it must be pork, for no other meat takes the flavor of wood smoke as does pork. Which brings us to the second thing: it must be cooked over wood coals, preferably hickory, although oak, pecan, or even apple will do. It must be cooked long and slowly, too—that we also understand—so that the juices are retained as the fat drizzles out, and so that it becomes tender enough to collapse at the touch of a fork. The final thing that North Carolinians understand about barbecue that few others do is that it must never, *never* be drowned under a heavy tomatoey, mustardy, or molassesey sauce, which only kills the taste of the meat. No, North Carolinians know instinctively that barbecue demands a light sauce that enhances the meat's smoky flavor with a slight vinegary tang, with perhaps a hint of red pepper, tomato, or sugar—but only a hint.

I must point out that there are two distinct schools of barbecue in North Carolina, however—Lexington and Eastern, with Lexington-style predominating in the Piedmont, Eastern-style from Raleigh to the coast. And while there is considerable argument about the two styles within the state, they really aren't as different as some of their proponents like to think. For Lexington-style, only shoulders of young pigs are cooked, while Eastern-style employs the whole pig, split down the middle. The Lexington-style sauce (they call it "dip") has a touch of ketchup and sugar, while the Eastern-style sauce is saltier and spiced with more red pepper. In the east, the meat is almost always chopped or minced. In the Piedmont, it is served chopped, sliced, or hunked. There is one more difference, and that brings us back to slaw.

Barbecue is always served with slaw in North Carolina and always has been. It cried out for a complementary side dish; cabbage was plentiful and cheap, and the sweet tanginess of slaw melded beautifully with the smoky flavor of the meat. Three different types of slaw are served with barbecue, and they are defined by color. Eastern-style comes with white slaw (made with mayonnaise) or yellow (to which a little mustard has been added with the mayonnaise), while Lexington comes only with red slaw (made with ketchup, no mayonnaise).

Originally, barbecue and slaw were served with some form of cornbread—hush puppies, cornsticks, fried johnnycakes—but with the advent of sandwiches, it was quickly made portable, served on slices of white bread, or a bun, always with slaw. And that, I suspect, is how slaw came to be traditionally added to hot dogs, hamburgers, and other sandwiches in North Carolina.

As further evidence of my proposition that North Carolina cuisine is built around slaw, I need only point to North Carolina's second most distinctive dish: fried seafood, fish camp–style. Fried seafood can be found in many places and many cultures, of course, but as with barbecue, North Carolinians just seem to grasp the concept better than others. We understand that the secret to fried seafood is light breading and quick cooking. This type of cooking also is called Calabash-style, for the little one-time fishing village near the South Carolina line where a group of seafood restaurants began to clump back in the thirties, although the style of cooking was common all along our coast for generations before that. The coastal restaurants that served these heaping platters of fried fish, shrimp, oysters, and scallops were so successful that entrepreneurs copied them inland. In the beginning, many of these places were situated near rivers or other bodies of water and were called fish camps, thus the term *fish camp–style*. Immensely popular, restaurants of this type proliferated away from water and continue to do so to this day.

Like barbecue, North Carolina's fish camp–style seafood needed a simple, complementary side dish, and there, of course, waiting modestly in the wings, was slaw. It was perfect, light and tangy and refreshing. Order a fish sandwich anywhere else in America and it will come, perhaps, with tartar sauce. Order one in North Carolina and you automatically get it with tartar sauce—and slaw. Only one bite of each is required to establish that North Carolinians have more refined tastes than anybody else.

The question that arises is whether slaw was served first with seafood or with barbecue. I don't pretend to know and leave that for others to debate. It is enough that North Carolinians saw its possibilities and employed them wisely.

We North Carolinians love our barbecue houses, our fish camps, our old-time hot dog and hamburger stands, and during the times I was away from home, I could find no substitutes. I found myself longing deeply for a chopped tray from Swicegood's at Fair Grove south of Thomasville, a sliced sandwich from Jimmy's across the street from city hall, a Skeenburger all the way from the Morning Glory next to the train station, a heaping platter from Midway

Seafood over toward High Point by the drive-in theater, longing so deeply, and with such a gut-wrenching fierceness, that I knew I would never be able to survive for long beyond North Carolina's fair borders.

And while none of those places I just mentioned still exists, I only have to drive a few miles from where I now live in Randolph County to Wayne Monk's Lexington #1 for a big tray of the world's best barbecue, or to Capt. Tom's Seafood over near Ramseur for a heaping platter of fried flounder, shrimp, oysters, and scallops, or to Johnson's in Siler City for the juiciest and tastiest cheeseburger on the planet—all served, naturally, with slaw.

And so I have remained at home in North Carolina, my belly and me, full and content. And may it ever be.

*The recipient of two National Headliner Awards and two Ernie Pyle Memorial Awards during his days as a journalist, **Jerry Bledsoe** is the author of twelve books, including the* New York Times *number-one bestseller* Bitter Blood. *In 1989, he founded Down Home Press, which primarily publishes nonfiction books about the Carolinas and the South.*

ELIZABETH COX

All I Know How to Do

My house sits on a hill, with a wide

apron of yard. One large willow tree stands beside the road, and up toward the house a hammock hangs summer and winter between two oaks. My children and the neighbor children play football in the yard. The hammock can hold five small children at a time.

When my daughter is a teenager she asks me to come out and lie in the hammock with her. She tells me what bothers her. Sometimes late at night I go out alone to watch the moon.

North Carolina is my second home. I have lived here more than twenty years and raised two children. My first home was in Tennessee, but I left at age twenty-one to get married. This fall I will marry again and leave North Carolina for Boston. I will move only part of my belongings, and I'm wondering what to take.

From where I stand I can see my mother's

sofa, which she always covered in flowered material. I covered it with huge chintz roses. I keep the Duncan Phyfe secretary in the corner and a bookcase near the door. On the wall opposite the window hangs an ornate gold mirror next to a Vermeer print of a woman in a kitchen. All of these things are my mother's. I keep her cranberry afghan in a basket beside the sofa. The room looks different from other rooms in my house, more formal. Nobody comes to sit here, though I come every morning to wait in my mother's nest. My brothers defined one end of the sofa as her nest. She surrounded herself there with magazines, cross-stitching, bowls of cereal and lists. In lamplight her white hair became a halo.

But her nest does not become my nest, though when I stand back I can see her there, and all I left at twenty-one. My Tennessee home sat on a hill in a circle of mountains next to the river. My home now is on a hill, but I only imagine the river.

One day while riding my bike down Garrett Road I realized I had been in North Carolina for twenty years. On that spring afternoon I stopped to speak to old man Garrett. He is a tobacco farmer, but with a mule and hand plow he plants one small space beside the road. I ask if I can plow a row and he allows me, grudgingly. The job is harder than it looks. I plow a wavy row, plow another, and he has to skip a wide space to correct my mistake and make it straight. The next day I see him with a black man as they haul manure on a cart and fertilize each row. They have huge shovels, and this time I do not ask to participate. All summer, as I pass the corn, I see evidence of my work.

During summer vacation I drive my children from Durham to the beaches or mountains. We bring back shells or pieces of gold from mountain streams. We put them around the house, but I keep one room that still has my mother's furniture, where no one except my brothers feels free to sit.

This past winter I created a new room by enclosing a porch. From the porch I look out into the woods where I keep two bluebird houses. The bluebirds come in droves—first to check it out, then to build a nest. They raise their young and let me peek into the nest to see eggs that are also blue and to see fledglings grow through different stages. When they are almost ready to fly I no longer dare to look into the nest. The mother goes to a nearby branch and calls to her young. She refuses to feed them until they come out. The small heads peek from the hole of the birdhouse, protesting. One by one they fly off. They are gone, and I feel bereft. I do not know if there are bluebirds in Boston.

The light in the South is soft and hot and foggy. I cannot imagine waking to anything else. The trees are fat and heavy, and so are many of the people— not lean like New Englanders. I try to think of how it felt to leave home the first time but cannot remember. My children are grown and gone away but they say, "You're not going to sell the house, are you?" They are creating homes of their own but do not want to think of this one gone.

"You can come to Boston," I tell them. They doubt it.

I will take my hammock to Boston, so that when my daughter comes there we can lie in it and talk or my son and his wife can spend an afternoon looking up at the sky or the man I will marry can stretch out when he comes home from the city.

Boston has busyness and a smell that moves me outside the nest of the South. I walk through streets of downtown, then go to surrounding towns and seek out ponds and streams. I try to make the place a part of my body. Gaston Bachelard in *The Poetics of Space* speaks of nests as a primitive sense of well-being. He describes himself in front of a fireplace during a storm as a creature huddled up to itself and "endowed with a sense of refuge." These movements, he says, are engraved in the muscles. He says we must know the psychology of muscles. Eudora Welty speaks of place as "the heart's field." Again the place becomes a part of the body.

If I take the hammock where all the neighbor children have played, where I have watched the moon and seen the change of seasons, maybe a huddling of my own muscles can be refuged.

The man I love lives in Concord, Massachusetts. Our new house will be in an area not far from Walden Pond, in Emerson's and Hawthorne's New England, their "heart's field." My house is a block from Walden Street, a few blocks from the cemetery of famous graves, a few miles from the river. There are two large willow trees in the backyard, where the hammock can go. The house is thin and proud with its Spartan rooms. The space around the house is narrow and neat. I have a room upstairs that is mine. Unfurnished as yet. Through the tall windows light comes in with complete fullness.

I will bring ocean shells and gold rocks from the mountains and something from my mother's nest. What I love moves me from place to place through my life. At twenty-one I left home and got married. At fifty-one I am leaving home, to get married.

One friend tells me, "It's all you know how to do."

*A native of Tennessee, **Elizabeth Cox** lived for twenty-five years in Durham, where she taught creative writing at Duke University. The author of two novels and numerous short stories and poems, she moved to Massachusetts in 1994. She continues to teach each spring at Duke. She has recently completed her third novel.*

LAWRENCE NAUMOFF

· ·

The Heart Pines

Because I've combined building houses with a

career as a novelist, a lot of what I've seen of houses and families and men and women ends up in my novels.

A lot doesn't end up in them as well, as what I see sometimes is a complete book in itself, with a beginning and middle and end, tragic or comic, always an end.

When my new book is soon published, I will have had five novels published by good New York houses. Before I was writing these books, and afterwards, I built or added onto or renovated more than fifty homes.

It's not the homeowner who used to come to the site at night with his cheap aluminum three-foot level and ball of twine and stretch strings down the sides of walls and across the bottoms of rafters to try to assure himself that his ideas of the perfectibility of wood and mankind alike were being fulfilled, or the homeowner who used to secretly add in changes and extra costs to the job and then plead with me not to tell her husband (please don't tell him, she'd say, he'll be so mad) and ask me then to hide the new costs somewhere, that I should write about.

It's not even the time I built a house for Reynolds Price, who would come over and with his pure, steady eye put the gaze on the latest we had done, and good-naturedly pronounce it plumb or not, and be right, so much that we took to calling him The Human Level, that I should tell.

And it's not the time the husband built a fifteen-hundred-square-foot addition with an art studio and another bedroom (for whom, we wondered, even though we thought we knew) because his wife said she was suffocating in the marriage and the children were driving her crazy and she needed her own space, and then, after he went into debt building it, she divorced him, threw him out and got the *whole house all to herself*!

Nope. It's none of those.

It's the house I built in the late seventies. It's the one I most often think about.

This architect-designed home was for a family moving to North Carolina from the Midwest. The husband was retiring at the age of fifty-five from his executive position, where we, who were earning at the time somewhere between $5 and $10 an hour, discovered he was making $150 an hour, which was real money back then.

He and his sparkling, hardworking, antique-collecting, artistic-minded wife had four children.

They had been working with the Chapel Hill architect for five years on the plans for this house, and it was given to me to build at whatever reasonable cost it would take, and there were no contracts, and we all trusted each other, and they would stay in the Midwest while I built it and send the money down, while I sent the pictures of the progress back up to them.

The house was to be thirty-three hundred square feet, which was considered pretty large back then (now everyone's a millionaire, it seems, and has a mansion), and would tuck in against the forest behind it and overlook the pond below.

The middle of the house was three stories tall, and all open. Standing beside the rock fireplace and chimney, on the first floor, you could see up the entire three stories and out the high windows. The floors ringed the open space with balconies.

There was a two-story cathedral-ceiling greenhouse built within the south side of the house. Its floor was red tile on concrete, and its entire wall was windows and sliding doors for at least twenty-five feet wide and twenty feet or more high.

There was a twelve-foot-wide Kalwall skylight in the roof, and the whole effect was to be able to grow tall plants and have a solar gain simultaneously.

The interior was all C-and-better V-groove pine with exposed beams in the ceiling.

The flooring, top and bottom, would be resawn heart-pine boards from beams from a two-hundred-year-old mill torn down in Savannah.

The wife loved to cook, and she loved her kitchen. We built in two four-burner JennAir ranges and ovens, as well as a Thermador convection oven.

They had a climate-controlled wine room (we had to build the racks—what a tedious and maddening job), and stained-glass windows they had collected over the years were given to us to install here and there.

I was building everything myself. I used the scrap left over from the flooring to build the heart-pine kitchen cabinets. We had as few subs as possible, and mainly they were for the mechanical aspects of the house. We did the cypress siding, the bookcases filling every wall of the library; everything was hand-done down to the toilet-paper holders which we designed (I know, who cares, but the design was nifty and smooth and oddball all at once).

Because they wanted me to do everything myself, the house would take some time. They said they'd be patient.

The family moved down, and while the children could probably have cared less about the looks and beauty and wonder of this house, and the husband, newly retired, paced back and forth and began to slowly go nuts from nothing to do, the wife visited the site and fell in love with the home of her dreams, the home she had helped design and bring to life over the five years of its creation on paper and in her heart.

Soon after, I received notice the beams had been milled into flooring. I decided I would minimize the risk in shipping this wood by sending one of my carpenters and a truck to pick it up. He and his Australian sheepherding dog left on Friday morning. On Monday, we unloaded the wood. We stacked it carefully to avoid splintering or breaking off the grooves where the tongue would bite once we put it down.

We rented two flooring guns and hammers. The boards were long lengths, which made the work go faster. It went together easily, proving it had been milled well.

The color of the wood itself was stunning. It was auburn and brown with streaks of yellow, almost yellow ochre, throughout, and in a few days the house changed from being an interesting, sunny and dramatic structure to having a soul. It became not exactly sensuous, but rich and vibrant and inviting.

Three days after we began laying the floor, the woman who had dreamed all this up, the wife of the pacing man and the wild and brainy children, returned to the job.

She became so quiet when she entered the house and looked at the floor that we stopped working and became as quiet as she.

She removed her shoes. Barefooted, she walked on the new floor and then, while we stood far away, across the house, watching her see this flooring for the first time, she lay on her belly on the floor and put her cheek to the wood and laid her hands out to the side, as if embracing it. She was still for so long we had to go back to work.

I suppose it had all come together for her then, all the work and all the vision and determination and good will she had given to this house, all quietly returned to her like something loved at a distance, or something once lost, like someone who had been exiled and now was home, it seemed to us that she was home.

In a few years, only a couple, maybe, I don't remember now, she died in her sleep at the age of fifty-one.

She had only a few weeks earlier discovered she had lung cancer, and somehow, as if in knowing it, as if in having it made real by the words spoken, as if in the knowledge of such horror being within her, she began to fail, and one night her lungs hemorrhaged and she died in the strangely, rustically lovely cedar bed which was in the house she had dreamed, on the floor she had loved, now her home.

It falls to us, then, to understand this structure we call the house, which becomes the home to the human spirit that creates it, which becomes a part of the life of the people within, which becomes the visible, earthly domain of our days, the site, then, where lives and loves and birth and death all reside along with us as purely as the streaked yellow ochre of the heart of pine, it becomes this dream of the house as home we incidentally celebrate in building, that she celebrated so in her act of embrace.

Now the children are grown and married and scattered across the state and nation. I've just been asked by the youngest child to build his own house for his new family. I'm sure I will. Of course I will. The spirit of his mother is in his face. I can see her in his manner, in his eyes, in the tone of his skin and in his passion for life.

Her vision and her dream still remain with this house above the pond with the dock and the fruit trees now mature and bearing and thriving, as are her children. In a way, it's for her I'll build it. In some way, it is.

Called by one reviewer "the Tonya Harding of Southern Literature," **Lawrence Naumoff** *(who can't decide if that's a compliment or not) has had four novels published. His forthcoming novel, which he says is his most outrageous and visionary, is called* A Plan for Women.

FRED CHAPPELL

· ·

The Possibility of Paradise

Among the traditional settings in which

fancy places the poet, the garden is the most attractive. There at least the verse maker can do little harm. He will not be inciting youth to revolt or troubling the opposite sex or scandalizing his proper neighbors. He will only be gently pleasing his senses, and writing, and sometimes—probably despite himself—thinking.

For the garden invites thought; reminiscence, surmises and sweet longings come to the mind like hummingbirds to the trumpet vine. Though the garden may contain some of the choicest parts of the world we live in, its lushest grasses and most vivid blossoms and brightest waters, still it is set apart from the world. Even in the cheeriest countryside the pleasure garden is still a place apart, a more precious space, where the savors of seasons are augmented, where the soul is invited to invite itself.

In this regard the poet's garden is no different from anyone else's. Here we all retire so that our fevers may subside and our frets quicken, and the poet retires here for the same reasons. But he may also come to his garden to read and write, in hope that the breeze that moves the branches of japonica and trembles the delicate white bells of the scilla set along the flagstone walk may freshen his pages and quicken his lines.

If the poet is in the slow process of composing a poem, he may like to imagine that his outdoor setting will impart to his phrases the earthen flavor of a loaf of bread that has been set outdoors to rise before baking. He may be sorely deceived in these fantasies; it is possible to scribble flabby lines and to think silly thoughts in the most ideal of settings. But since the writer is likely to be deceived about the value of his work anyway, why shouldn't he choose a pleasing place to enjoy his deception?

I find myself writing these lines on a fine spring morning, and our garden surrounds me with its green light and seals away the noises of the busier world as securely as if I were seated on a lake bottom. Actually there is a fair amount of noise from neighborhood cars and trucks, but there is no sound of television, no boom-box rap music, no buzz of motorcycles. It is interesting to note how the removal of only a few of our contemporary irritants makes a peaceful difference in one's state of mind.

It is still early spring—the dogwood petals show almost as much green as white—but there is bloom. The maroon-and-burgundy pansies in their urns have wintered well and are glad for the milder season. The hard little berries of mahonia are colored a dusty emerald. There are bluebells and fancy streamers of japonica as white as fresh laundry, and in the far corner where the board fence traps the warmth a few red azalea blossoms have undertaken their adventure toward glory. This garden is young as yet and boasts no tall camellias, but I can enjoy my neighbor's as they lift scarlet above the fence.

I have been referring to the poet as "he." This is not thoughtlessness on my part, or mere chauvinism. I believe that male and female writers enjoy different kinds of relationships with gardens. Some of the best male literary figures who write of gardens are Sir Thomas Browne, Francis Bacon and Henry James. I don't believe that any of these men ever so much as grasped a spade or pruning shears. It defeats my capacity to try to picture the ponderously elegant Henry James on his knees before a fern.

The best women writers who treat of gardens are Colette, Edith Wharton and Vita Sackville-West. Each of these women was a hands-on enjoyer. Sackville-West was heroic in her incessant quest for the most hospitable walkways and most tumultuous flower beds. Colette thrust her hands into the soil to help seal the heart that had been a thousand times broken and rebroken. The women made their gardens; the men were given theirs.

And in my case this is also the fact. My wife, Susan, helped the landscapers to design our garden and to lay it out. It was she who oversaw the construction, imagined the possibility of a wall fountain and transformed the old pump house that serviced a vanished swimming pool into a fantasy hut decorated with designs taken from ancient astronomical treatises. My chief contribution to the building of the garden was to grumble about the racket the backhoe made. I think that Francis Bacon and Henry James would have done the same.

Can we find here a difference in the male and female imaginations? I dread to venture into suppositions that may be seen as political in our days, yet I will submit that the woman writer has a firmer understanding of the intimate materials of the world than a man does. A man enjoys admiring a garden; a woman enjoys primping it. Men who devote extraordinary time and effort to improving their looks are seen as vain, but women who do so are known as wise and prudent. Perhaps a woman sees her garden almost in the way she views herself, believing that no matter how generous Nature has been in giving her beauty there is always opportunity for improvement.

I might try to brush these shaky speculations from my mind, except that I realize that the garden has inspired them. Poets generally are not such able philosophers as their friendly critics make them out to be, but in a garden even a bibulous love-poet is likely to turn thoughtful, to muse upon the possibility of paradise, the nature of eternity and the presence of God. Then when he returns to his familiar themes—Beaujolais and blondes, let us say—he may find that his happy lines have taken on a deeper tone than he has achieved before.

For the garden inspires romantic love as well as the more intellectual kind. Shakespeare delighted to place his lovers in gardens. There they played chess and discoursed gravely or gaily about the serious matters of the heart. There they sang songs and constructed elaborate practical jokes and made fantastic wagers that soon became serious enough to reveal their characters and the soul of the age they lived in.

Even the language the lovers spoke to one another was a botanic tongue. They spoke of lady's-slippers, heart's-ease, love-lies-bleeding and rue, of forget-me-nots, of bride's bonnets and lady's-tresses. They wore flowers in their hats, scented their breath by chewing green leaves and sprinkled their clothes and shoes with crushed herbs. An Elizabethan lady or gentleman was likely to be an ambulatory garden, distilled to its essences.

They were smarter than we are. They understood the value of having some reminiscence of the garden about their persons. They knew that the experience of the garden can be both private and social at the same time and that the garden is the place to speak of intimate topics while retaining a smiling courtesy. They courted one another as pleasantly and intelligently as they could devise to, and after a proper space of time became our ancestors. The twilight spread over them, and the nightingales began to sing.

In our own garden this morning the birds are singing and two cardinals are playing tag, dipping from oak to birch to oak. I must suppose that they too are courting. The day will be warm, and though rain is promised for next week Susan is laboring at watering the plants. They are as grateful for her ministrations as living things can be—and so am I. As I see her move with her gleaming watering can from shrub to shrub I feel as watchful as the clematis buds that sway on the trellis.

A native of Canton, North Carolina, and a Duke University alumnus, **Fred Chappell** is the author of two new books, Spring Garden: New and Selected Poems and Farewell, I'm Bound to Leave You. He teaches English at the University of North Carolina at Greensboro.

SIMMONS JONES

· ·

A Charlotte Childhood: My Life As a Genius

I first found out I was a genius in Charlotte

in the year 1926   when I was six years old. This agreeable news was revealed to me by several remarkable women in two completely different, remarkable structures. One was the building in which I attended school, and the other was my grandmother's house. On the strength of this information, I made plans to get out of town at my earliest possible convenience and head for New York City and Europe.

New York City and Europe were the two places I had heard spoken of that sounded good enough for me to emigrate to—probably never to return. Certain glorious people I held in high regard had gone to New York City to go on the stage and to Europe to study art or dancing and speak in foreign tongues. It seemed to me that a genius should be able to do one or all of these pleasant things without too much resistance from non-geniuses. Obviously, at that time, I had had no instruction in the sweet uses and convenience of money.

I went to primary school in what had been a hospital for wounded and dying soldiers in the Civil War. It was, as I remember, an imposing brick building as permanent as the pyramids, with nothing remaining of sickness or death. Its rooms were full of light and beautiful, old lady teachers who adored me and told me almost daily that I was a genius. These same ladies had also taught my mother. However, they had not told her she was a genius, which I could certainly understand. I was their "little dreamer," because I spent the better part of every day gazing out the enormous windows at the trees that were, in those days, always in full leaf. I don't know why this gazing was taken as a sign of genius, except that it was in a more generous age, when an unsatisfactory child was assumed to be exceptionally brilliant. I was very unsatisfactory. However, it was on the day when I read out to the class my first complete sentence, as my teacher pointed to the syllables on the blackboard, that I confirmed to myself and all present that I was privy to a superior world.

When school was dismissed at the end of the morning, an aunt or a cousin or a cousin's nurse often came to fetch me, and we would walk the three or four blocks to my grandmother's house, which I understood to be the actual real world of my life. It did not occur to me that all the other children in my class did not have their own complete, dreamlike worlds to return to when the bells sounded through the halls, bringing that part of the day to an end.

My grandmother's house had started out as an Italian villa with a square tower and a balcony over the entrance. It had been built by her father some years before the turn of the century—late enough so that there were vast interior bathrooms and early enough so that every bedroom had a fireplace. However, my grandmother, a woman of creative dissatisfaction, chose to look back to an earlier civilization and had the tower cut off and a Greek Revival facade imposed onto what had been the rear of the house, so that it faced a pleasanter prospect and a more amiable neighborhood. Its rooms were full of light and beautiful, eccentric aunts who adored me and told me almost daily that I was a genius. In the afternoons, I produced boisterous plays on what had become the back porch, and I was observed in rehearsal by my aunts through the tall windows. They were thunderstruck by my brilliance.

Eventually, at age fifteen, I did manage to emigrate—well, actually, what happened was I was sent away to various schools, where I excelled and failed as I pleased, and later on I went off to war and after that to New York City and Europe for the better part of a lifetime, as I had predicted that I would. There were no beautiful, old lady teachers or eccentric aunts in any of these places to reassure me and lift me above the crowd. Being a genius turned out to be a grave disappointment. As a matter of fact, I was recognized as such much less frequently, if at all.

After many years, I returned to Charlotte, as I had never thought to do. I found a town that had changed character and taken a new and more determined direction. The Civil War hospital and my grandmother's house had been razed, and in their place were monstrous structures of rectangles and parallels and multiple crossings of numbered interstate highways, desperate with rushing traffic, and nothing remaining of any civilization of more serene intent. The beautiful teachers and eccentric aunts had vanished from the face of the earth without a trace, except for a certain light in the eyes of their aging pupils and of their pupils' children and even sometimes of their grandchildren.

Sometimes now, as I drive through the dusk on out-of-the-way streets in forgotten neighborhoods, I come across a house, elegant and dim, looking out from behind its trees with an air of indifference. If the lamps have been turned on in the windows and the curtains not yet drawn, I delay for a moment, hoping for the shadow of a familiar figure against the light. However, even the quiet streets do not allow for too long a pause, and I am reprimanded from behind by the shrill, mechanical voices imported from Germany and Japan. I move on, reluctant and dissatisfied.

I live now in a remarkable structure, thought of as fashionable almost three-quarters of a century ago and now fashionable again, less so, of course, but still imposing in the middle of a town which changed its face and has changed its face again. Its rooms are full of light and the ghosts of the remarkable la-dies from my youth. They appear now and then and sit in these rooms where ornaments from their lives—a chair, a book, a mirror—have begun to be at home with me. Phrases from the past whisper in the air, urging me to finish what I began on my travels, urging me to continue the journey outward. It is my duty to obey, so far as I am able.

Recently, I have been struck by my great good fortune to have had my start in those rooms radiant with voices of enlightenment and imagination. I have long since understood—and with considerable relief—that I was not in any way a genius, nor was I ever thought to be. I can see now that when those extraordinary women called me "dreamer" and "genius," they had recognized with their long-distance X-ray vision that I was destined to follow the path of my life outward, a life probably too careless and full of error, but nonetheless the only life I could have lived.

And surely, if I could hear their voices now, they would welcome me back home again as the beloved emissary, chosen by them to make the journey they could not make themselves, due to custom and the purpose and obligation of their gender.

*Born in Charlotte in 1920, **Simmons Jones** has lived in Rome, Paris and New York City, where he worked as a freelance photographer and helped produce plays on Broadway. His first novel, Show Me the Way to Go Home, was published by Algonquin Books of Chapel Hill in 1991. According to Simmons, "This novel should be played on an upright piano, slightly out of tune, and very late on a summer night with all the windows thrown open."*

PHILIP GERARD

Down to the Sea

We always drove to Cape Hatteras at night. The

first time, I was a teenager, traveling with neighbors who had vacationed there for years. Later, in college, I drove my own hard-used vehicles—an International Scout, a Datsun pickup. Years after that, my bride, Kathleen, and I spent our two-week honeymoon there in a cottage without a telephone.

From Delaware, it was four hours of fast traffic to the long tunnel-bridge across the Chesapeake. South of Virginia Beach, the traffic thinned. Three hours more to the summit of the Bonner Bridge—Oregon Inlet shining below in the moonlight. As we slid down onto the north end of Hatteras Island, a palpable sense of relief would wash over me.

Sanctuary.

At the crux of the island, Cape Point Campground awaited with cold outdoor showers, indoor bathrooms, and a sandy lot where we could pitch our tent. But no matter how late it was, we always stopped at the lighthouse first.

Usually, it was past midnight. The breakers would be thrashing onto the beach—invisible in the darkness. The rotating beam of Hatteras Light would compass the sky, sweeping twenty miles out to sea. There was nothing quaint about it: the lighthouse was a stark obelisk rising from a barren spit of land in a dangerous sea.

So why have I always felt such safety, such peace, in so precarious a place?

Maybe the question is its own answer. There is something reassuring about standing at the edge of things, where land meets sea, reckoning the boundaries all over again. Having the metaphor of our precarious existence made literal to the regular, soothing rush of the breakers.

Literal: *littoral*. Where the sea meets the land. That's how I think of it.

I was born into adulthood on Hatteras Island.

After two years of a soul-stifling Catholic high school, I ran away to Cape Hatteras and lived in a tent for a whole summer, waiting for college to begin. That summer, I carried my life in an orange backpack—jeans and shorts, T-shirts and flannels, extra sneakers and clean socks, poncho, red one-quart Palco canteen, Swiss army knife, Primus stove, Boy Scout mess kit, packets of evaporated milk and cinnamon-raisin oatmeal, and Marine Band harmonica in the key of C. Strapped to the pack was a twelve-string Gibson guitar in a hard case. My tent was a sky-blue nylon A-frame that cost twenty-six dollars at J. C. Penney.

I rode the Amtrak to Raleigh. The air conditioning in the coach broke down in Baltimore, and I was delayed three hours, so I arrived in the dead of night. As I walked the dark street from the station past the closed iron grates of seedy storefronts, a burglar alarm sounded and police cars materialized out of nowhere, and cops swarmed out of them, guns drawn, and rushed one of the buildings.

I kept walking, hoping nobody would notice a lone vagabond, then hitchhiked out of town. I slept under the stars in a field and woke to the head-lights of a Highway Patrol car trundling slowly across the field toward me, its spotlight sweeping the tree line. The lights stopped at the foot of my sleeping bag, and the biggest trooper I'd ever seen shined a flashlight into my face, played the light across the pack, the guitar case, and shook his head.

"You carry all that on your back?" he asked in a voice more full of curiosity than menace.

"Yes, sir," I said. I'd learned early to be polite to cops.

"Heading for the beach?"

"Yes, sir."

He checked my driver's license. "You won't have any trouble catching a ride," he said, then got back in his cruiser and drove away.

By next afternoon, I was pitching my tent in the salt breeze.

That summer, I shared camps with a succession of neighbors. There was the van load of surfers from Florida, who rose at sunup to catch the big waves that swelled and broke on the lighthouse jetty, then slept through the after-noon in the shade of a tarpaulin rigged to their Chevy van. In the evening, they'd trade perfect-wave stories while lounging inside on the purple shag carpet, listening to eight-track tunes by Led Zeppelin and the Beach Boys. They taught me to surf—sort of—on a ten-foot board, what they called a "log." It felt dangerous and exotic, but I was not very adept.

Another group consisted of the whole crew from a beef-and-beer joint in Baltimore. Their leader was a blond man in his thirties who wore an extraor-dinary moustache, and their headquarters was a M*A*S*H-style army surplus tent with a ridgepole like a circus "big top" and roll-up sides. The furniture consisted entirely of cases of beer—stacked into platforms for sleeping, chairs for lounging, tables for playing cards and eating. As their two-week stay wore on, the furniture gradually disappeared, leaving a vacant floor.

They passed through all summer: a blues guitar player from Virginia, col-lege kids from Connecticut, fishermen from Omaha, drunken rednecks and honeymoon couples, church-camp kids and tourist families, old hippies from everywhere. Every night, we built a bonfire below the high-tide line on the beach and passed around the guitar, drinking Boone's Farm apple wine and iced beer, and sang the night away. In those days, everybody seemed to know all the same songs—standards by Woody Guthrie, Bob Dylan, Doc Watson, Pete Seeger, Peter, Paul and Mary, the Grateful Dead, the Allman Brothers.

I slept every night on the ground, watching the stars through the mosquito mesh on the front flap of my J. C. Penney tent. Through many days of brain-scrambling heat and many nights of cool, distant stars, I learned to watch and listen and pay attention to the world.

It was a good summer to be on the road, and, because the island was so full of other strangers, it was a fine place to be a stranger.

America: named for a navigator, Amerigo Vespucci, who mapped our coast five hundred years ago. In Latin, the language of the Church: *Americus*. Though we celebrate wagon trains, cattle drives, and prairie home values, we are an island people. We have made of America an island—bounded by two oceans, the chain of Great Lakes, and a shallow river. The mountains couldn't stop our "Manifest Destiny," nor the desert. We stopped at water.

Our native English literature contains a catalogue of watery tales: *Moby Dick*, Jack London's *The Sea Wolf*, Ernest Hemingway's *The Old Man and the Sea*. It's hard to find a writer of stature who has not written about voyages in boats: open boats (Stephen Crane), tall ships (Richard Henry Dana), speedboats (F. Scott Fitzgerald—remember the green light on Daisy Buchanan's dock that tantalizes Gatsby so for all those pages?), even research boats (John Steinbeck's *The Log from the* Sea of Cortez).

Boats are, after all, just floating islands, peopled by the ambitious, the desperate, the kidnapped, the cast away—the sort of interesting folks writers love.

Living in the Sonoran Desert of Arizona, I dreamed Cape Hatteras alive onto the pages of my first novel, *Hatteras Light*. The desert landscape was oddly familiar—the subtle nuances of blended color in the late-afternoon shadow;

the brilliant periwinkle sky, hard and clear as bottle glass; the roiling purple violence of storms that sweep out of the distance full-blown and take your breath away, then disappear in a moment, leaving the air scrubbed clean.

But like the landscape, I was missing water.

It always seems more profitable to write about a place when you are somewhere else. Maybe it's that you have to imagine it harder—envision it more completely, ponder it more deeply. Part of why you write about it is that you yearn to be there.

But of course it doesn't really exist. The place you create on the page—the island I imagined into a novel, the island I am recalling now from that long-ago summer—never really existed at all. It was always at least partly a mirage, filtered through dreams and experience. I found there what I needed to find. You would have found something altogether different.

Memory is its own country, with constantly shifting borders and characters who move in and out of focus, changing identities, combining, all talking at once, even if they've never met.

So I created my own Hatteras from memory, and I peopled it with folks like the ones I had known there, and I put most of them in small boats. They were lifesavers. They dared the big water. They oared their wooden boats through the breakers and out to the edge of the world, and they came back stronger, and with the deep, troubling wisdom born of elemental struggle.

The abiding mystery of big water has fascinated better writers than me, especially novelists. In a novel, as on the ocean, the reader can navigate across a visible surface, out of sight of the known landscape. In the depths beneath it lurks danger.

Where the sea meets the river, we frequently find our best literature. Mark Twain's *Huckleberry Finn* and *Life on the Mississippi*. Joseph Conrad's *Heart of Darkness*—told by Marlow, remember, to his fellow passengers as their ship languishes at anchor in the Thames estuary waiting for the turn of tide. A ghost story, a parable of evil ambition, a story of a quest up another river into the blackness of the human heart.

We are a nation of harbors: New York, San Francisco, Chicago, St. Louis, Baltimore, Miami, Boston, Philadelphia, San Diego, Los Angeles, Galveston, Seattle, New Orleans. Through those harbors have passed immigrants and slaves, indentured servants and refugees, all of them offering something of value. America is a brawling waterfront, a chaotic trading market of new ideas and fresh perspectives. Our national paradox is that we are both a free port for ideas and a fierce island of isolation. Our national anthem is the heroic ballad of a harbor defense.

I live now between the Cape Fear River and the Atlantic sea. Not exactly an island, but a place of many waters, of tides and weather, a place where nature is not abstract but actual, a live presence that affects everything we do here.

To know this place, you have to see it from the water—the light is different, softened by haze, and an unfamiliar skyline rises out of the routine camouflage of the land life. Things look different from out there, bobbing around in the whitecaps, or sliding along through the oily calm of a November drizzle. It smells different. A biologist friend tells me she loves the stink of low tide on the oyster flats. "Smells like life," she says.

I spend as much time as I can on the water in small boats. Whenever possible, I sail, because then the rush of wind and water is not masked by the diesel groan. The shoreline on this coast is not dramatic, like the headlands of California or the rocky cliffs of Maine. It is more subtle, a low coast with very few landmarks. Offshore, you can't see where an inlet is unless you know already where to look for it. The shoaly bottom shifts, channels are scoured or filled in, often in the course of a single storm.

You have to pay attention.

To notice the change of seasons in the marshes and tidal creeks, you have to look harder—bright greens shading to pale greens then to wheat browns, hiding ospreys and herons. This coast is the edge of everything—not a sharp crease between worlds, but a boundary where one thing turns gradually into another, dry land into wet land and finally pure water. A miracle of the most subtle kind.

In our veins runs salt water—literally. Or, *littorally*.

The surge of breakers on sand pulls at the sea within us like a great magnet. We are drawn to the edge of water. We can watch it for hours, mesmerized. The great sea makes us feel insignificant, but it calms us. It puts our ambitions in perspective. Unlike a mountaintop or a vast desert, it moves. In our pulse, we feel the rhythm of the sea, the quiet heartbeat of a live planet.

They say that iambic pentameter—the favorite meter of Shakespeare—mimics the human heartbeat. Then the sea is poetry. And like all great poetry, it enlarges us. Fills us up with wonder and possibility. And when we leave it, we carry away its music in our ears, and in our hearts the quiet thrill of being human.

At the edge of water, on the most exposed point of land along a low coast, we raise a lighthouse—to warn us, and to beckon us.

Philip Gerard misspent his youth hitchhiking across America. He once crossed the Mojave Desert with only a sixteen-ounce can of warm Olympia beer for company. Now, he stays as close to the water as he can. He is the author of three novels and two books of nonfiction, most recently Creating Nonfiction: Researching and Crafting Stories of Real Life. *He directs the Professional and Creative Writing Program at the University of North Carolina at Wilmington.*

TIM MCLAURIN

. . . .

The Rite Time of the Night

The stars twinkle like millions of tiny campfires,

the splinters of light sharp in the cool April night. I pause on the back deck and admire Orion, hanging high in the sky. Mars is climbing through the boughs of trees; the war god's red eye is as cold as the glint of a sword edge as it blinks between tender leaf blossoms. I scratch the dog's ear, and he whines and thumps his tail against the boards. I have enjoyed the night sky since I was a child and first began to read about the constellations and planets. I wish for a moment my two children were not sleeping and could join me and watch for the trail of a meteor. I pat the dog's head and walk inside.

I go through this ritual every night—closing up the house and making sure the dogs are fed, the porch light turned off, the door locked. By habit, I like to sit up till midnight, and by then my wife, Katie, and

109

the children are long asleep. Wallace, our 120-pound mastiff, guards the outside of our home, but I must patrol the inner rooms. Opening the refrigerator door, I take out the children's lunchboxes, which Katie packed earlier. Turkey-and-cheese sandwiches, Fruit Roll-Ups, Sippit juice boxes and small sacks of potato chips—the kids say they don't like school lunches and always beg to bring theirs from home.

Back when I was in grammar school, taking your lunch was a sign of poverty. On the few occasions my mother was short the necessary quarters, I tried to hide my brown-paper sack. I check the stovetop and oven, sweeping the dials twice with my eyes. The dripping water faucet is turned off. The thermostat must be set a hair above seventy.

My parents followed a similar ritual, but in a place much different from our ranch-style house in Chapel Hill. I was raised in the country, near Fayetteville, in four rooms, with wood heat and no indoor plumbing. Mama worried with banking the fire in the stove just right so the coals would smolder, setting the chamber pot in the light of the hallway.

I sit in the recliner and begin to remove my shoes. Through the window, I see streetlights and garage lights surrounding our home like a constellation fallen to earth. I think about the land we are wanting to buy—ten acres several miles out of town, on a ridge covered with hardwoods. No streetlights out there, only the glow of fireflies in warm months and foxfire burning in felled tree trunks decades in decay.

I check the children next. Meghan sleeps in her single bed, the floor and walls cluttered with the things of little girls. When I was eight, all five of us siblings shared a room. I tuck the covers under her chin, and she turns from her back to her side. Her kitty sleeps at her feet.

I remember the time my father brought home six baby opossums when his coonhounds killed the mother in a hunt. They were uglier than rats. We fed the baby possums milk from a doll bottle. At night, they would crawl from their cardboard box and climb into bed with us and sleep tucked under our chins. We eventually released them. I don't want Meghan sleeping with possums, but I regret she does not have the access to nature I was privileged to have. I kiss her warm cheek.

Christopher's room is next. He sleeps on his stomach, doubled up with his rear end in the air. I turn him on his side and adjust the covers. Earlier tonight, he told me he wanted a BB gun for his birthday, and I told him he'd have to wait until he was twelve. I wonder at my double standard, for I owned my first Daisy air rifle when I was nine, the gun bought with money I earned in the tobacco fields.

I recall how the robins would arrive in late February. In twin holly trees in our backyard, the birds would gather by the hundreds to eat the red berries. My brothers and I, armed with slingshots and the air rifle, would slay the fat birds by the sackful. We'd bring the meat proudly to my mother, who would cook it with rice. Maybe if we buy the land, I'll let him have a rifle a couple of years sooner. There, he will be distant from neighbors' windows and cars. Christopher rolls back to his stomach and doubles up. I pat his bottom and leave him to his dreams.

The door to our bedroom creaks as I open it, but Katie does not wake. I undress by the window's glow, then slip under the quilt into the warm folds of our waterbed. My eyes slowly adjust to the dark until I can just see the ceiling light, the dresser against the far wall.

We have been in this house for five years. It seemed like a mansion when we moved in. Christopher was only days old. We had been living in a tiny apartment we rented after returning from the Peace Corps in North Africa, where I had once again lived without indoor plumbing. But the food was spicy and good and the people gracious. Our American standards had diminished in Tunisia, and this house seemed too big for only four people.

From the four-lane boulevard that runs close to our house, I hear the drone of late-night traffic. When I was little, the sounds of night were frogs and crickets, dawn punctuated by the coo of doves and crowing roosters. I worry that my children will come to associate morning with the increased roar of traffic from the boulevard as people hurry to jobs.

Katie's sleep breath whistles through her nose. She has always liked horses, but she grew up in Memphis and only rode occasionally, at boarding stables. We owned a couple of ponies and a workhorse when I was small. We'd fashion bridles from baling twine and ride bareback through the fields.

Katie and I have talked of buying a horse if we purchase the land. A friend who is a farrier has pledged to help us find a mare or gelding gentle enough for the kids, yet with enough spunk that Katie can gallop with the wind blowing in her hair.

Banks, down payments, hocking more of our future toward working for pay. But families grow in both body and vision, and what we once believed to be the center of the universe shifts to the frontier. All of us carry in our hearts the best memories of childhood. A father should not be faulted for wanting to visit upon his children the morning coo of doves, if at the same time he provides them the tools to build the foundations of their own lives.

Tim McLaurin, *the author of* The Acorn Plan, Keeper of the Moon *and* Woodrow's Trumpet, *is a former marine, Peace Corps volunteer, carpenter and skilled handler for a traveling snake show. He lives in Chapel Hill.*

ROBERT MORGAN

The House Place

One of the memorable events of my childhood,

maybe the most memorable, was the building of our new house. We lived on the Green River in Henderson County, North Carolina, on land bought by my great-great-grandfather Pace in 1840. First we lived in the old Morgan house down by the river; then, when I was three, after the death of my grandma Levi, we moved into the old Levi house at the foot of Meeting-house Mountain so Mama could look after my grandpa Levi.

From as far back as I can recall Mama had talked about building a new house. Daddy resisted the idea, partly because he wanted to move back to the Morgan house, which he owned, and partly because he had no money to buy materials. He hated to work jobs for wages, even though he was a skilled carpenter and mason and house painter, and he made so little growing pole beans, his only money crop, that he could not afford a truck or car or tractor, much less a new house.

But it was Mama's dream, almost an obsession, to own a new home. These were the years immediately after World War II, when building was starting up again and new things seemed possible. She began to put all the money she could save, five and ten dollars at a time, in the post office in Hendersonville. She saved quarters and dollars from selling eggs and butter, from selling her chickens. When we were truly broke she returned to the cotton mill nearby and worked for a few weeks or months and added what wages she could spare to the savings account in the post office. By the late summer of 1949 she had saved seventeen hundred dollars, and she decided it was time to begin work on the new house.

"Why do you put money in the post office?" my sister Evangeline asked her.

"Because the bank might go broke," Mama said. "But the post office never goes broke."

I remember going with her to pick out the site for the construction. It was in a stretch of woods above the road, between the Levi house and the church. It was on a piece of property Grandpa Levi had given her. There was a kind of opening in the trees, where sunlight played on the moss and leaves of the forest floor. I had gone there to rake leaves for cow bedding with Grandma Levi when I was two or three. The rusting springs of an old cot stuck through the leaves. My uncle Robert, who had been killed in the war, used to go up there to sleep on summer days after working the third shift in the cotton mill. Spots of sunlight through the trees roved over the ground.

Every night after the supper dishes were washed Mama worked on her drawing of the projected house. Sometimes she consulted with Daddy and sometimes she consulted with Grandpa Levi, who had been a builder. But I don't think they believed the house would ever be built. Mostly she worked on her own, using a pencil and a ruler on a sheet of typing paper. She drew closets and erased them. She added a bathroom and laundry room to the design, and three bedrooms, a dining room and living room. "The kitchen will be right here where it catches the early sun," she said.

Daddy sat by the fireplace reading the paper or *National Geographic* and ignored her plans most of the time.

The worst quarrel Mama and Daddy ever had was in the late summer of 1949 when Daddy came home from the bean market one evening with a new rifle. It was a Winchester .30-06, a rifle he had wanted for years for hunting deer on the government land. He had spent $275 on the rifle, all his profit from the pole beans that year. Mama was so furious she screamed at him, and then wouldn't speak to him for several days. He had promised to put his earnings from the field in the post-office account but could not resist the temptation of the new rifle.

Perhaps it was Mama's anger that spurred her into action. One afternoon the next week, while we were visiting my aunt Wessie at her house across from the church, a great truck loaded with a bulldozer roared into the churchyard and stopped. As we looked on, the driver of the truck climbed up on the bulldozer and started the engine with a blast; then with a lurch he drove it off the flatbed and out the dirt road. We followed the smoking machine.

Turning below the house place Mama had picked out, the bulldozer reared up the road bank into the woods. We came running, and I saw the machine crash through the woods, knocking down saplings and pushing big trees aside. Its tracks creaked and clanked as it hit one tree trunk after another. The driver parked the bulldozer in the little clearing and left. I went up to the big machine and rubbed my finger across the thick shiny blade. Diesel smell filled the woods. I climbed up into the seat and held the levers as I had seen the driver do.

The next morning I heard the engine roaring in the woods even before I got out of bed. As soon as I had eaten my grits I ran through the woods to the site and stood beside Daddy as he watched the bulldozer work. Big trees had been knocked down all around, and a wide shelf had been carved out of the golden dirt and red clay of the mountainside. The bulldozer backed up and lurched forward, pushing a crumbling foam of soil. The driver raised the blade and pushed over another oak that came whooshing and cracking down.

The clay shone like it had been polished where the blade cut it. Diesel smoke filled the woods, and trees pulled out by the roots were piled at the bottom of the clearing. When the site was level the bulldozer backed up and began scraping a trough where the cellar would be. It cut a hole six feet deep and pushed the dirt to the edge of the clearing. Last, it graded a driveway that swung around the lower edge of the clearing to the road.

I could hardly believe the mountainside had been torn open that way. The quiet spot in the woods could no longer be recognized. What had happened was thrilling and scary.

That fall I played every day in the dirt that had been opened and shaped by the bulldozer. I climbed on the piles of dirt and the stumps with roots flung out like spider legs. I ran down one side of the cellar hole and up the other side. I watched as Daddy and Uncle Arthur drove stakes and stretched string to outline where the foundation of the house was to be. They dug trenches for the footings. I helped mix the mortar to be poured in the bottom of the ditches.

One day Uncle Arthur smelled like he had been taking medicine, and his face was red. When Mama came up to the house place with her drawing plan she found he had laid off one side of the house only half as long as it should be. Uncle Arthur was so embarrassed he said he wouldn't charge her anything for that day's work. He and Daddy laid off the north side again, adding the part where the kitchen was to be.

Daddy hired a cousin with a big truck to help him cut white oaks on the mountain and carry them to the sawmill to be cut into lumber. I'm sure he chose oaks instead of pines because he thought the oak planks would last much longer.

An even bigger job was getting rocks out of the river and creek for the veneer of the house. Both Mama and Daddy were sure they wanted a "rock house," not of cut and dressed stone but of creek rocks fitted together in irregular shapes like pieces of a puzzle. Daddy got into the river with an iron pole and pried rocks loose, choosing those of the right thickness and wrestling them to the bank. He selected rocks for variety of shape and color, for contrast and texture, flint and quartz, granite. When he had assembled several big piles on the bank he brought the horse and wagon down to the river and carried the rocks to the house site. Those he got out of Rock Creek several miles up the river he had his brother-in-law carry in his truck.

The rocks were heaped around the periphery of the clearing. I played on the stacks so much I got to know each of the rocks with its special color and shape before it was ever put in the wall of the house.

One morning that fall I awoke to another roar in the woods up near the house place. I got dressed and ran across the field and through the woods in time to see a huge truck back into place at the upper edge of the clearing. It was unlike any truck I had ever seen. On its bed was a furnace with a chimney and a big boiler with pipes coming out of the top. And leaning over the whole truck was something that resembled a narrow cage with a wheel at the end of it.

"What are they doing?" I said to Mama.

"That is McCrary, the well digger," Mama said.

I watched as they parked the heavy truck and jacked it up level so the back wheels were way off the ground. Then they started a fire in the furnace, and steam began coming out of the boiler. Soon the furnace was roaring, and they raised the long cage with cables until it was a kind of tower on the back. The cables ran over the pulley wheel on top of the derrick. They fastened a big bar on the end of the cable and drove a pipe into the ground at the back of the truck.

When the man turned the motor on steam hissed out the top and the cable went up and down, clanking ta-ta-*ta*, ta-ta-*ta*, ta-ta-*ta*. Another man poured water into the hole they were making. I could hear the clanks echo off Cicero Mountain. They drove in more pipe, and more pipe, and then they pulled the cable out of the hole, and I saw the thing on its end was like a long tin can that spewed soupy mud onto the leaves below the hole. The mud was not red but gray. They kept pouring in more water and spewing more mud on the leaves. The mud ran down the mountainside. The men twisted new pipes into the hole with wrenches big as plows.

All day I heard the well digger go ta-ta-*ta*, ta-ta-*ta*, as I played back at the house. The next day when I returned to the site the man holding the cable hauled up the long hollow can and offered me a drink of water. "There is a river down there," he said. He opened the flap at the end and clear water gushed out, but I backed away.

The next day they put pipes in the well, long silver pipes that swayed and rang in the air as they twisted them together and lowered them into the bigger pipe. Grandpa and Daddy watched as they fitted the long thin tubes into the well. When Mama came up from the old house to see what they were doing she gasped, "But I asked for copper pipe."

"Ma'am, there hasn't been any copper pipe since before the war," the well digger said.

"The contract specifies copper pipe," Mama said.

The well digger looked at Grandpa and then at Daddy. "They said the iron pipe would be okay," he said.

"Then get them to pay you," Mama said. "For I'm the one that has the money." She turned and walked away.

The well digger appealed to Daddy and Grandpa, but they had to admit that Mama had saved the money and kept it in the post office in her name. With his face red and his voice trembly with anger the well driller told his men to start pulling the galvanized pipes out of the well. The next day he brought copper pipes he had found in Asheville.

For Christmas that year I was given a small tool set. The tin box held a little saw and hammer, a level and coping saw, a ruler and small plane, a try square and tape measure. It may have been the most important gift I have ever been given. All that winter, as Daddy and Uncle Arthur laid the rock foundation and nailed the sills and joists together, I watched and worked nearby. As soon as there was scantling and blocks and scraps I began to borrow nails from the bags and boxes and hammer together toys. I nailed slats on two-by-fours to make biplanes like the crop duster that swooped down on the bean fields in summer to lay its trail of pungent fog. I whittled propellers with my pocketknife and rounded a rudder. I mashed my fingers again and again and scratched myself with the saw.

On cold mornings I stood by the fire Uncle Arthur had made at the edge of the work site. His breath smelled sweet as fuel, and his face was purple as he held his thick hands out to the flames. I watched the plumbers as they roughed in the pipes. They had a little stove that roared its blue fire beneath a bowl where they melted chunks of lead to soup. They used blowtorches like paintbrushes to spread the drips of solder around joints.

Soon as my own hands were warm I went back to hammering. I made a big airplane with the motors turned backward like those on the B-36 I had seen in *National Geographic*. With pointed blocks of two-by-fours I made speedboats like those I had seen on Lake Summit. I even tried to make a well-digger truck with a tower and a wheel at the top. I sawed out wheels from saplings for little cars and trucks. I knocked together birdhouses and tables that might go into a dollhouse. "Help us stir this mud," Daddy said. I took the hoe and raked it back and forth in the mortar box to keep the cement wet and soft. But soon as I was free I returned to my own building.

As the joists and beams were nailed in place on the house I tried to nail fins on a stick to make a rocket. The things I constructed were bare and bland and rough, but I saw them as colorful and glittering. While I hammered the actual wood I saw it mostly in the imagination. Uncle Arthur gave me a little hatchet with which I sharpened the bows on boats and the noses of airplanes. I even made a little bulldozer with a blade that could be raised. I felt intimate with the wood, with the grains and textures and possibilities of each different piece.

By late winter Mama had run out of money and Uncle Arthur no longer worked at the house place. By then the subfloor had been put down at a cross angle and Daddy was beginning to put up the frame of studs. When the rain came it soaked the subfloor and the upright cage of two-by-fours. Water stood in the cellar hole. All the work had come to a stop. There was no more money, and besides, Daddy had to start plowing if he was going to put in a crop. The house site looked harsh and chaotic around the lattice of studs. The piles of dirt bled in the rain, and leaves fell on the canvas over lumber and the heaps of rocks. Puddles stood in the dirt around the foundation.

This began a pattern that lasted over the next several years, as Mama and Daddy worked on the house until they ran out of money, then waited months until they could start again, after the farming season was over or after Mama had worked in the cotton mill again or as a clerk at the J. C. Penney store in town. Whenever I went to town with her I had to spend hours hanging around Rigby-Morrow, the building-supply store near the railroad tracks, while she discussed prices and financing with the sales clerk.

When visitors came on Sundays and holidays we always took them up to the house place and showed them what had been done. Mama explained how the house was going to look when finished, and what she planned to do next. Daddy was defensive and nervous when he showed another carpenter what he had made, maybe because he was only a part-time carpenter.

"Why, Clyde, you're going to have a ten-thousand-dollar house," Rafe Huggins, the foreman from the cotton mill, said to Daddy as he looked at the construction.

During the second winter, after Daddy already had the frame up, he tore the metal shingles from the old Morgan house and hauled them to the new house place in the wagon. He stacked the shingles like the pages of an iron book on the bank above the site. Suddenly Mama ran out of money again and couldn't even afford nails. "I can't put the roof on without nails," Daddy said.

"I ain't got but ten cents," Mama said.

"Then get a dime's worth of nails," Daddy said.

"I'd be ashamed to go to Walker's Hardware and ask for a dime's worth of nails," Mama said. At that point Daddy broke down and wept. It was the first time I had seen him cry, and I felt as though my bones were seared and crushed.

By the summer of 1951 the house had a roof and was covered with tarpaper. It would be years before the rock veneer would be finished. But Mama began to talk of moving in. Some of the rooms still needed Sheetrock, but the Celotex ceilings had been put in and the sink in the kitchen worked. Duffy Corn came every day for two weeks that summer and made cabinets out of plywood for the kitchen. There was a feeling of imminence and gathering momentum. On rainy days when Daddy couldn't work in the fields he labored in the new house. We talked as though our lives would be completely different once we moved into what we still referred to as "the house place."

If I left something scattered on the floor Mama would say, "I won't let you do that when we move to the house place. Everything will have to be kept neat there."

In the new house all would be clean and shiny and working. Mama had ordered an electric stove and a refrigerator. We would be happy and more responsible, better people. We would invite the preacher for Sunday dinner in the new dining room. We would hang our stockings at Christmas on the stone mantel taken from the old Morgan house. Daddy had brought the hearth rock from the old house also and placed it in front of the fireplace in the new living room.

Mama decided we would move in before school started that fall. For days we carried bags and boxes up to the new house. But on the day of the move my uncle brought his pickup truck to carry the furniture. He and Daddy drove back and forth all that hot August day, loading and unloading bedsteads and mattresses, tables and bureaus. We walked up the trail across the field and through the woods, carrying pillows and tablecloths, quilts and pots and pans. It was a day of exuberance and tension. It was a threshold. This was what all the work and worry had been building up to. From now on our lives would be changed. The pride Mama and Daddy showed was shared by Evangeline and me.

Near the end of the day we had moved nearly everything that needed to be moved. Mama made her last trip and then stayed to fix supper on the new electric stove. She had never used an electric stove before. I still had to go back to the old Levi house for my pet chicken called Hembo. I kept him in a box on the back porch. The sky had clouded up and it was about to rain.

"Here, put on your raincoat," Mama said.

As I started back through the woods in the heavy raincoat the storm began. It was a cold late-summer rain, and as I hurried through the field the wind threw the drops in sheets and gusting veils. At the old house I gathered up my pet chicken and put him under the raincoat. He was my best friend, and all that summer I had played with the yellow biddy with an orange beak, letting him run across the floor, stroking his fuzz with my finger, talking to him like a confidant. Hembo was my companion as I sat in the hot sun dreaming vast dreams those summer days. I had taken him to play with me in the field above the orchard and in the meadow beside the branch.

Holding the chicken under my coat I ran up the wet path to the new house. But when I got there and put Hembo on the clean floor he fell over, limp as a wilted flower. I picked him up but he fell over again.

"What's wrong?" I said to Mama.

"That chicken is dead," Grandpa said.

"He must have smothered under your coat," Mama said.

I couldn't believe Hembo was dead. I kept touching him and turning him over, expecting him to rouse and walk away.

"Put that bird outside and wash your hands," Mama said.

All through supper at the new table I continued to glance out at the door-step to see if Hembo had waked up.

The rain stopped about the time supper was over, and the sun came in through the new windows. Evangeline and I took Hembo out into the woods to bury him. We dug a hole with a spoon under a dogwood and placed the biddy in it. After covering the grave with dirt and leaves we heaped daisies and wild roses on the mound. Then we sang a hymn in the dripping woods as late sun lit the drops in the canopy overhead.

I have one other memory of moving into the new house. I think it was the next day, after we had slept the first night in the new bedrooms. Daddy came back late from the bean market. We had already eaten supper when my uncle's pickup drove into the yard. Evangeline and I ran out to see what Daddy had brought. Sometimes he got a watermelon at the market after the beans were sold. The truck rattled and idled as Daddy lifted something down from the bed. In the twilight it was hard to see what it was.

And then we recognized that it was a new wheelbarrow, a deep mason's wheelbarrow with a fat balloon tire. "What is that?" Mama said from the doorway. As my uncle turned the truck around and drove away, Evangeline took one handle of the barrow and I took the other, and we pushed the vehicle around the driveway. We pushed it past the piles of lumber and the heaps of rocks with leaves on them. We pushed it into the woods and back.

"Be careful," Mama called.

I climbed into the bed, and Evangeline pushed me across the yard until the wheel hit a root and turned us over.

"Are you hurt?" Mama called.

We righted the wheelbarrow and ran it over the sand pile. Then we danced around the vehicle.

"They are as tickled as if I had bought a truck," Daddy said.

In the gloaming woods and yard we drove the wheelbarrow over rocks and piles of dirt, over pieces of lumber. We were living in the new house and we had a new toy. I ran and leapt onto the sand pile and landed on my behind with a jolt. I have never felt such exuberance since.

Born in the Blue Ridge Mountains of North Carolina, **Robert Morgan** *grew up in "the house place." The author of several books of poetry and four works of fiction— most recently* The Truest Pleasure, *published by Algonquin Books of Chapel Hill in 1995—he has taught creative writing at Cornell University since 1971.*

MARIANNE GINGHER

A Heartfelt Home

Because I am one of a vanishing species

of adults who continues to live in the town

where I grew up,   I have visual access to my former childhood homes. Despite commercial encroachments, all four of them survive, updated and well maintained. At least two, by current market standards, are as pricey as castles—neither my parents nor I could afford to buy them today.

The house that in the early 1950s played host to our rowdy tumble has since been owned by quiet retired couples and gives me such a cold shoulder when I drive past it that I'm certain my family wore out that dwelling's patience the same as its rugs. Renovations to the first house we lived in have so gussied up its original simplicity that, with its flowery wrought-iron railings, it looks embarrassed—like a plain woman sporting a grandiose hat.

I have returned to only one of these

houses—by invitation—and felt oddly displaced. I behaved the way I behave at high-school reunions: gushy about change, when change rarely feels any better than compromise. I'm afraid that I sat pining for evidence of my long-scattered family in rooms that were no longer meant to please or accommodate our quirks.

In retrospect, the houses of our childhood seem more like guardians, living, breathing relations, than forms of shelter, and, returning to them, we dread witnessing their adaptability. To discover that our secret hideouts have been claimed for another's purposes makes us feel not only dispensable but betrayed. Knowing a house well, forming an attachment to its atmosphere and spirit, is one of our earliest experiences with intimacy.

It's that intimacy with place—the sense that a house will share with us its secrets as well as its blessings—that we long for as adults and that we seek to recapture in the homes we eventually buy. Why are the houses of our adult lives never quite as influential as the ones that nurtured us as children? Perhaps, because we are responsible for their mortgages and upkeep, we view them more as burdens than sanctuaries. Creating a feeling of hominess is a conscious task; we just don't fall into the feeling the way we did as children. What does make a house a home? Perhaps only a child can tell us—or memory.

I've been growing up in Greensboro since about 1950, when my father, a native North Carolinian, returned to settle. For a while, we lived on Aberdeen Terrace in a small, rented two-story white frame house. The house had a grumbling coal furnace that my father patiently stoked each morning before he went to work. This was the house that had fig trees in the backyard. There was a boy in the neighborhood named Rudolph Gibbs, memorable because he had a name like the famous reindeer and a sister, Carolyn, whom my mother was always praising for her good manners. The Aberdeen Terrace house is the one in which I recuperated from red measles, my fever cooled hourly by alcohol rubdowns. My baby brother received shots of gamma globulin there—words that still spook me and glob in my mouth. I would have rather suffered the measles than those shots.

We owned our first TV on Aberdeen Terrace. I remember watching *I Love Lucy* while my mother vacuumed. I remember the vacuum cleaner: it resembled a bomb being towed by a sled.

That was the home where I slept with my entire record collection every night. My father recalled that when I tossed in my bed, all the records clattered out, making such a racket that he often shot up in the dark, thinking he'd heard burglars. I remember that I had a little plastic tote in the shape of a pumpkin that I set on one of our heat grates and that the pumpkin melted. I don't remember my mother getting mad. Mostly, she sang a lot and kissed my father while they did dishes.

I loved the neighborhood there. We had sidewalks and lots of trees. There was a crab apple tree and a pussy willow. There was a boy who took his pet rabbit on walks. Around the corner lived a couple who trained little dogs instead of children and taught the dogs a repertoire of tricks. The dogs had even better manners than Carolyn Gibbs. Mike Cole lived across the street. Both he and his mother talked like they had head colds or maybe adenoids. I liked the word *adenoids*, although I didn't want them. Some people had theirs taken out, like tonsils. It was a popular operation, a remedy of some sort that's rarely performed today. It seemed back then that somebody was running for president named Adenoid Stevenson.

We didn't live in the Aberdeen Terrace house for more than two or three years, but I retain a strong impression of its borrowed, dogeared grace. I recall that the house faced east, and the front rooms were butter colored in the morning, their windows swagged with white nylon curtains as thin as cobwebs. The hardwood floors were splintery and warm. There weren't any rugs; you could take running leaps and slide a long, long way in your socks—or if your pajamas had feet. A staircase ascended to a landing where I liked to sit, peeking through the knobby balustrade, and spy down at the adults.

Mother was glad to leave Aberdeen Terrace. "That house was cramped," she often said after we were gone. But I don't remember it that way. I remember it as offering me plenty of space for dashing and tumbling and whooshing down the banister. At night, in the dark, the house felt so big that to get to my parents' bedroom in the wake of a nightmare required the dogged courage of a pioneer.

I loved the comfort of that house. It wasn't the sort of house anybody acted nervous or prissy about. It catered specifically to my rambunctiousness, and its familiarity, like soft flannel, provided the sort of nurture that belies shabbiness.

Our second home, which my parents built, was in a lush new suburb called Starmount Forest. I remember going out to the lot to tag trees we wanted the bulldozer to spare.

The yard was spacious, like a small, shady park, with room for a swing set, a playhouse, a dog lot, a lemonade stand, kickball and croquet games and my mother's snapdragons. I remember the yard almost better than the house. I was in the heyday of my tomboyhood, and the house alone could not possibly have contained my daredevilry.

I had my own bedroom in Starmount Forest. The walls were painted salmon pink, a color I will forever associate with privacy because I discovered the joys of such, holed up in my bedroom, writing my first stories and saturating myself with Nancy Drew and Lois Lenski books.

In this house, I feasted on Saturday television: Roy Rogers and Hopalong Cassidy and Wild Bill Hickok and Sky King, the flying cowboy. We watched television in a dark little den on a small black-and-white set that was always missing its tuning knobs because some child had wrenched them off.

The years spent in Starmount Forest were dominated by invention. My first bowl of snow ice cream was eaten there; the best Halloween costumes I ever wore were assembled by my mother there; a picture window was in the living room, and on frosty mornings, we scratched elaborate murals with our fingers on the glass; one Christmas morning, we found sleigh bells that Santa had dropped in the front yard—my father verified their authenticity. We turned the swings of our play set into superlative horses, using bath towels for saddles and my father's silk neckties for reins.

On moving day, I remember that I ran dramatically from room to room in a swoon of regret, kissing every wall good-bye. The house had always felt like a land of plenty, and we had not expected to leave it any more than my mother had expected to have another baby.

To accommodate our increase, my parents built what they referred to, after every meeting with the architect, as their dream house. Everybody expects to live in one eventually, and my parents were no exception.

It was tremendous, crowding its small, treeless yard with a cool, classic elegance we were always a little uncomfortable with. The house didn't seem to need us. Despite our noisy numbers, we couldn't seem to fill it up. The big, square rooms, some of them tiled in linoleum to cut costs, seemed to echo the disappointments of dreams falling short. There was too much dependence on overhead lighting, rather than lamps, so that the house never felt cozy. It glowed with the high, dry, cheerless light of motel rooms.

Still, there was poshness and convenience: an intercom, an asphalt driveway as black and shiny as patent leather, a built-in charcoal grill beside the stove, acres of cantaloupe-colored Formica in the kitchen, two fireplaces, central air, a laundry chute, a spiral staircase, walk-in closets far grander than my salmon pink bedroom in Starmount Forest.

We tried to liven up the place a bit. My brothers invented a game whereby they dressed in football helmets, strapped pillows around their chests for padding, then shot one another down the spiral staircase in cardboard boxes like makeshift bobsleds. We spooked each other with ghostly wails over the intercom late at night. For a biology project, we turned one of the walk-in closets into a lab and raised, etherized and dissected white mice.

Still, the house shrugged us off. The cherry tree my father planted in the front yard as a memorial to his own father died. My parents kept postponing buying furniture for the living room—perhaps the earliest sign that they had built beyond their means. After we'd moved to the old, genteel, weathered house in Sunset Hills, I overheard my mother telling a friend that attempting to decorate the dream house had been like trying to furnish Mammoth Cave.

I was seventeen when my parents bought the white two-story brick house on the corner of Ridgeway and Madison in Sunset Hills. The real-estate agent had encouraged my parents to think of the house as "having possibilities." A bargain, it was in desperate need of renovation and repair. On moving day, my mother sat in the hallway on a pile of unpacked crates and wept.

But for all its dilapidation, from the moment I saw this house I knew I was home. How did I know this? Tall and handsome, tucked in a grove of towering oak trees, the house possessed both charm and dignity. A little ragged around the edges, sure, but it was a house that was not ashamed of its history. Its stairs were garrulous with creaks; the hinges of its doors and cupboards sang squeaky songs. There was a glass pantry and a carved mantel and frosted windowpanes in one bathroom. The walls were of cool, fragrant plaster. Outdoors, a flagstone path meandered through old-fashioned plantings that one's grandmother might have tended.

Something about the house, something sunny and possible, reminded me of our beginnings on Aberdeen Terrace, when my father had not complained about the necessity of shoveling coal, nor had my mother fussed over my pumpkin tote melting on the heat grate. This house in Sunset Hills, settled and worn, overgrown and outgrown by the family before us, felt patient—that's what it was. It was in no hurry to be anything other than what it had always been: a graceful shelter, a house to come heartfelt home to.

On the day we moved in, before she'd unpacked the first dish, my mother wiped away her tears and strolled around the living room, picking out the spot where the Christmas tree would stand. It was August. One normally did not think of Christmas trees then. But my mother was thinking of them. The house spoke to her, she said, and told her that thinking of Christmas trees and where to place them would cheer her up.

You always know that you are home when a house speaks to you—and they do speak, the best of them.

I was told to take a spin down the long, curving banister, and even though I was seventeen, I could not resist such a friendly invitation.

Marianne Gingher, who teaches writing at the University of North Carolina, is the author of two books of fiction. She lives in Greensboro not far from the houses in which she grew up, in a 1920s bungalow with a kitchen her grandmother would feel at home in: no microwave, no dishwasher—but there is a nifty, old-timey meat grinder.

FRYE GAILLARD

Back to the Land

I grew up in Alabama. Summers there were a

magical time, most often spent on my uncle's farm. It was a vast, exotic piece of land, two thousand acres of rich prairie, rolling eastward toward the Lowndes County line. White-faced cattle grazed on the hills, and every so often there were stands of pine that soon gave way to black-water swamps. On horseback, I roamed every inch of that territory, learning to ride with the help of old Mack, a swaybacked bay nearly thirty years old. He was an animal wise in the ways of young children, gentle and sure, not much given to stubbornness or fright. We scouted the range for outlaws and Indians, until one fine day on the strength of his teaching, our cowboy games gave way to the real thing.

The work was hard—long days in the sun chasing runaway steers, castrating newborn calves, vaccinating the herd against disease.

But with my uncles and cousins and the other hands on the place, we managed to find a little time for adventure.

One hot afternoon, for example, after a morning of rounding up strays, we went to fish at a pond behind the house. On the far bank, we saw an old canoe—a dugout that my uncle and his son had carved from a tree. There had been a storm the night before, and the boat had obviously blown loose from its moorings. It lay upside down in the mud, waterlogged and in need of repair. I agreed to paddle it back across the lake so we could pull it out at the dock. At worst, I thought, the canoe would sink, and I would simply swim ashore. But as I moved out sluggishly toward the middle of the water, I realized it was not going to be that easy. The canoe listed badly to the starboard side, and no matter how I paddled, it tended to veer in that direction.

I was cursing it silently under my breath when all of a sudden, to my absolute horror, a rifle shot rang out from the shore. The bullet hit the water not a foot from my boat.

"My God!" I screamed. "Have you gone crazy?"

"Just keep paddling," my uncle replied, taking new aim. I thought of diving for the safety of the water as a second shot thudded into the side of the canoe. But then I saw my uncle's target. Actually, there were multiple targets, for I had apparently paddled through a nest of water moccasins, and they were swimming purposefully in the direction of the boat. One, in fact, was slithering inside when the second rifle bullet split him in two. It was a situation so appalling, so completely terrifying and absurd, that it was hard for a moment to believe it was real.

I cursed again, then paddled furiously for the next several minutes, which seemed like days, while my uncle continued to fire away at the snakes. Finally, just as I thought I might have it made, the canoe ran aground thirty feet from the shore. Swept away by a new wave of panic, I jumped out and ran—my feet barely breaking the surface of the lake.

For years after that, my uncle told the story with relish, and it became enshrined as a piece of family lore—the day a mere mortal walked on water.

And so the summers unrolled through the years, with each new adventure a little more grand, until boyhood ended with a sudden jolt.

Those were dark and dangerous times in Alabama. In Montgomery, barely ten miles from my uncle's farm, the civil rights movement had begun to take shape, as a handful of preachers, eloquent and bold, launched their assault on the Southern way of life.

In the season of retaliation that followed, houses were burned, churches were bombed and people were murdered on the Alabama back roads. Families, once whole, were suddenly divided, and mine was no exception. Visits to the farm became less frequent.

And yet there was something about it that beckoned, some whisper of freedom in those wide-open spaces that, as the years went by, I wanted my own children to understand. For a long time, I tried to resist it, fearing disillusionment at the hands of a memory that I knew had only grown sweeter with time. But then one night in 1988, I was picking up dinner at a Chinese restaurant. As I waited in the lobby, I began leafing idly through a real-estate guide that some customer had recently discarded. On the last page, there was a picture of a farm—far less grand than my uncle's, for sure, but a rolling patch of land with a barn, a half-acre pond and a rustic farmhouse nestled in the trees.

At the time, I was living in downtown Charlotte, barely five minutes from my newspaper office. I liked urban life well enough and dreaded the thought of a lengthy commute. But the farm was only fifteen miles from the city, and my wife and I began to talk about it.

"Let's at least take a look," she said.

So we did and promptly bought it, and in the years since, we have learned a few things about living in the country. Most obviously, we've discovered the peace of going back—the feeling that comes at the end of each day when you leave the deadlines and glass-office pressures and turn at last down the rutted gravel road. In a way, I suppose, we are just playing at it. We lack the patience to be real farmers. But we have built our extended barnyard community—horses, dogs, a few stray cats—and we have seen our children explore for themselves some of the pleasures of our own childhood.

Just this morning, I watched as my youngest daughter, Tracy, set out across the fields on her favorite mare—a high-stepping sorrel by the name of T-Bird—flanked by Gretchen, her golden retriever, arguably the world's most exuberant dog. They have developed quite an understanding among them, a mutual delight in their weekend frolics—back through the woods or the pasture by the pond, where the great blue heron comes in the spring.

But there is something more substantial we've all discovered, more satisfying even than horseback rides or afternoon walks or the physical challenge of farm chores.

Here in the community of Indian Trail, we have learned again what it means to be a neighbor. It's a disappearing art in many urban settings. But it's alive and well at Larry Pressley's store, where the wood stove burns on winter afternoons and the farmers who come for their weekly supplies never seem to be in much of a hurry. There are jokes to tell, stories to swap, and every now and then somebody has a need.

I remember a couple of years back when Hurricane Hugo came ripping through, snapping pines and tearing old hardwoods loose by the roots. We all joined in to clean up the mess, and nobody was finished until everybody was. That's pretty standard in times of disaster. But then one day a few weeks later, my neighbor, Mrs. Lemmond, stopped me on the road.

"Mornin'," she said. "I reckon you knew Marshall fell out of that tree."

Good Lord, I thought, for her husband, Marshall, is a tall, thin man who is pushing sixty-five—not the right age for that kind of adventure. To make matters worse, it turned out that the tree he had fallen out of was mine, a towering oak near the end of the pasture. As Mrs. Lemmond told the story, her husband was worried about a dangling limb—a legacy of Hugo—fearing it would fall on one of the horses. He knew I was busy on a writing deadline, so he decided one day to get his own ladder and cut the limb down. The only problem was, when the branch came loose it took the ladder and Mr. Lemmond with it, and they all fell a good twenty feet to the ground.

Remarkably enough, he wasn't really hurt and hadn't thought to mention the episode to me. "No problem," he said, when I finally saw him. "Hope you didn't think I was trying to meddle."

That's the way it has been in Indian Trail. Good-humored generosity seems to be a staple, and for me at least, the feeling of community that comes out of that calls up memories of an Alabama farm. It's dangerous, I know, to sentimentalize. The rural South has known more than its share of suffering, and even today the old problems linger—poverty, racial prejudice and all the others that come in that package. But there has always been another side to it, a deeper understanding of the most basic ties: to land and family and the people around us. There may be understandings more important than that, but I'd be hard pressed to name what they are.

Frye Gaillard, former Southern editor of the Charlotte Observer, *is the author of twelve books, among them* If I Were a Carpenter *and* Lessons from the Big House. *A native of Mobile, Alabama, he lived for a while in Tennessee before coming home to North Carolina.*

HAL CROWTHER

Old Dogs Dream of Spring

Most newspapers run some kind of

nature column, a quiet corner of the

editorial page where a nameless disciple of H. D. Thoreau celebrates the changing seasons, notes the tides and the phases of the moon and rhapsodizes about dogwood, autumn colors and wild geese in flight. Sentimental and overwritten, in a style that resembles nothing else in the paper, the column is some tired editor's favorite sideline and most jealously defended prerogative.

It's been done well and parodied well, this genre. I wouldn't try to improve on it either way. But I remember a story one of my teachers told me in graduate school, about a new managing editor at the *New York World*, I think, who carelessly fired a little old man who for decades had published a few paragraphs of nature worship at the bottom left corner of the front page.

The old fellow poked around Central Park, mostly, noting what was blossoming or hatching or dying.

The new editor wanted to modernize his paper by eliminating tired features that had long since lost their readers. Within a week of the disappearance of this particular feature the *World* was inundated with protests and canceled subscriptions, and more angry mail than its editors had ever received on any issue. Within three weeks the Central Park naturalist was back in his corner of the newsroom and the front page.

Through all a newspaper's organized misinformation—the domestic news distorted by the prejudices and allegiances of the owners and editors, the foreign news shouted or whispered according to the often nefarious purposes of the government that supplies most of it, the numbing repetition of crimes and catastrophes, the overcooked ephemera of the sports pages—through all this compromised, tainted, all-but-useless information the readers somehow recognized the only news of abiding human interest: that the planet still supports life and that it still supports *your* life.

The reader knows this. Sometimes the writer forgets. Sometimes with deadlines pressing and outrages clamoring for my attention I temporarily lose this perspective.

That's when I'd take a walk with my dog. Not my dog exactly, more like my stepdog. Not a dog I would have adopted, purchased or chosen on my own. Of all the temporal and spiritual riches in my wife's dowry this beast was the item least likely to provoke envy. He was the product of the genetic whimsy of ancient Welshmen, who developed the stumpy breed to snatch badgers and then rebred them to herd sheep. It produced a versatile animal—if you needed help with sheep or badgers—but a shaky disposition. Noisy and cranky, this dog obeyed no commands unconnected to food or walking, his only loves. He was jealous and hateful toward small children, cuter pets and anything roughly his size that got more attention than he did.

In his prime he wasn't a great dog, and his prime was past. He howled neurotically at imaginary possums and still made an ass of himself over taller dogs in heat. Good looks had once been his strong suit, but now chronic skin infections kept him shaved bald from the tail halfway forward, a neo-punk effect that stopped tourists in their tracks.

Our relationship was a courteous standoff, most of the courtesy on my side. I built up credit in heaven by including this animal when I walked, even though he usually peeled off at the end to go back to the neighbors he preferred.

I knew he'd desert me this time, too, the little son of a bitch. But I included him on this particular walk, a kind of annual ritual between us, because it took us along the creek by the house where he'd lived when he was a puppy. He had taken his first walks here. He knew every stump, every sand bar and woodchuck hole. It would have been cruel to leave him home. I didn't really like him but I'd begun to empathize with him. Lately we had something in common, at last: neither of us was young.

It was the first perfect day of the season, here in Chapel Hill. This dog wasn't noted for expressing gratitude, but his pleasure was embarrassing. He rolled in the violets, moaned and slobbered. He herded imaginary sheep in short bursts of his best speed, but with a stiffness that told me I wasn't the only one with arthritis in the hip. The dog, delirious, almost forgot that he was walking with a loser. I promised not to compete with the newsroom rhapsodists. But it was that time in the Carolinas when dogwood and redbud compete with the first lime-green leaves; if you squinted to blur your focus what you saw were fragile clouds of green and white and violet floating through the trees.

It was, as Alan Paton wrote in the prologue to *Cry, the Beloved Country*, "lovely beyond singing of it." The woods along the creek were carpeted with blue phlox and white starflowers, and the short-legged dog was almost invisible running through the flowers, with a wave like a breeze passing.

It hadn't been such a hard winter here, though I'd begun my own winter in Eastern Europe, where they were sealed in an icy fog that stretched from the Danube to the Baltic. But it was a winter that took a heavy toll of our few great thinkers; Samuel Beckett died, and Lewis Mumford and Bruno Bettelheim. Irving Berlin and Judge Learned Hand, who had lived almost forever and seen a hundred springs, missed this one. A winter death that depressed me especially was Tony Conigliaro's, the luckless Tony C., the kid from Boston who could have been the greatest Italian ballplayer since DiMaggio. I saw him play in my hometown when we were both eighteen, when he played like an immortal. He died at the end of the winter after a life so blighted with disaster that Job would weep to hear of it.

My brother and his family had buried their old dog at the end of winter—a dog not much older than ours. My old dog and I were at an age and in a position to consider our mortality, and I at least took full advantage of it.

I looked around and thought, to hell with Eastern Europe. Around the next bend new leaves and apple blossoms were reflected in polluted water that only a dog would drink, and he did. Here was another path uphill through the redbud, and neither of us was tired. There had been better men and better dogs who didn't live to see all this, but we did. And no one watching us would have dared to bet that we wouldn't live to see it again. Name me something that doesn't pale beside such a blessing.

Canadian-born **Hal Crowther**, *already a veteran of* Time, Newsweek, *the Buffalo News and the Hollywood script mills, arrived in the Triangle nearly twenty years ago. His syndicated column originates in the* North Carolina Independent. *A collection of his essays,* Unarmed but Dangerous, *appeared in 1995. His wife, Lee Smith, says he is "real nice," though he has been called an "anger artist" for his fierce writing style, which has earned him the H. L. Mencken Award, among others.*

ELLYN BACHE

Coming Home

One of the first things I liked

about Wilmington was that in summer the women, no matter how horrible-looking their legs, did not wear hose.

This was a good sign, because I had been skeptical about moving from Maryland to North Carolina with four school-age children, to a place anyone could see was just a dot on the map many miles from anything except the Atlantic Ocean. My husband, Terry, said not to be ridiculous, the town was modern and thriving, why else would he move his building business there? But I feared it might be like when I'd gone to school in Chapel Hill in the early sixties, where the manners seemed formal and the accents foreign. Bare legs were hopeful, but what did they prove?

We moved anyway—on Labor Day 1985—to a rented cottage on Wrightsville Beach while Terry built our house fifteen minutes away in town. The ocean was warmer and calmer than in Maryland, and even though I was busy revising a novel and he was working long hours we managed to swim every day. In Maryland the weather would be chilly by now; in Wilmington it was still summer. We could sit on our beach towels, sopping wet, and never feel cold.

The children started school, people began to call. When our oldest boy got strep someone recommended a doctor, and sure enough he recovered right away. This was almost as encouraging as the bare-leggedness of the women. From the deck of our cottage we watched the water change color with the weather—Caribbean-blue in full sun, gray-green when clouds blew over, pewter when it stormed. The window in our bedroom gave us the sunrise, and in the evening the sun set over the marsh to the west, where long-legged birds fed as the sky faded to pink and purple behind them. It was all very exotic, and I was taken with it more than I expected.

Terry and I both had an office at home, and at lunchtime we ate together on the deck, where we found ourselves pointing to the sea and shouting at each other to look as the dolphins made their way south just beyond the breakers, arcing in and out of the water in their graceful ballet. Later in the day the brown pelicans would glide by, modern-day pterodactyls scanning the surf, dive-bombing in and out just as suddenly, beaks full of fish. Imagine! Tropical birds! In our front yard!

The beach was nearly deserted during those warm, sunny autumn days, but in the evening the surf fishermen came with their tackle and set to work. They were hardy folks who seemed to know what they were doing, and Terry was determined to glean their secret. "Casting out wherever the gulls feed—see?" he would say, watching intently. One day he bought some fishing gear and announced to the children that he was going down to catch our dinner. Fat chance, I thought. But he did, and that night we ate the blues he caught, and listened to him brag about his technique. It turned out to be beginner's luck, not skill, because he never caught a thing in that surf again, though he tried many times.

There was a hurricane scare in late September, and the children were delighted. Their classmates had filled them in on how, the year before, Hurricane Diana had ripped through Wilmington, tearing up trees and blowing off roofs. Their own stories of snowstorms couldn't compare. Jealous for having missed the excitement, heedless of our warnings that devastation was far from fun, they were hoping for a repeat. But Gloria teased, then blew north, and the next morning the dawn brought sunshine and Carolina-blue skies. "They called off school for *this*?" Then they went down to the beach and discovered the bounty the storm tide had brought in: enormous whelk shells, bigger than anything they'd ever collected. Almost as good as snow.

Along with the shells were papery necklaces of whelk egg casings, long beige leis. We slit open one of the linked segments and emptied it onto the table: dozens of tiny, perfectly formed whelk shells, not much bigger than pinheads. The children licked their fingers to pick them up, each shell pristine and hopeful-looking.

As autumn progressed the sun came at us from a sharper angle, the sea seemed darker, and the tides brought in a great wash of kelp and seaweed, which gave the beach a musky, fermenting smell, as if the whole ocean were composting, gathering for the coming cold.

But no cold came, at least not then. We discovered that we were living in an exotic pocket of mild air, where the occasional crisp day would be followed by a warmer one, and warmer yet: always the move toward heat. Our youngest boy went trick-or-treating in shirtsleeves, when in Maryland he had always complained about needing a jacket under his costume. We drove to the zoo in Asheboro, and were taught the lesson all newcomers learn when they move to Wilmington: that it is folly to wear summer clothes for trips inland and not carry jackets and flannels for the chill that prevails once you climb out of the protected coastal plain.

More than by the weather, the change of season was marked by the drawbridge over the Intracoastal Waterway, which divides Wilmington from Wrightsville Beach. Until November it operated sensibly enough, opening on demand for the few commercial rigs and just once an hour for the glut of pleasure boats. Then, precisely when the entire sailing community of the Northeast decided to move south for the winter, the rules changed, and the bridge opened on demand for any boat captain who asked. Sometimes it went up four times an hour, its cumbersome grids edging toward the perpendicular with grinding slowness, a seven-minute proposition. How we hated the bridge! Then our youngest pointed out that we must live in a castle—mustn't we?—because when the bridge rose to block the road it created—didn't it?—a moat.

By the time cool weather set in in earnest it was the new year. On the beach the mornings were frosty and the wind was fierce, whipping the sea oats around on the dunes, finding its way into every hidden crevice of the cottage. We were glad that our house in town was ready for us to move in.

In Maryland winter is a desolate season: dormant grass, the skeletons of leafless trees, a landscape of grays and browns that can be dreary even at midday. In Wilmington there are pines, magnolias, live oaks, lawns planted with winter rye. Bare trees: yes, those, too, but enough green to cheer the soul.

And sun! More light than there had ever been farther north, where the winter sky was dull and often cloudy, where the few pale rays that seeped indoors were sopped up at once by the furniture. In Wilmington I bought a cherry dining table and watched the Southern sun glint off the finish. I polished more than I needed to, for the welcome novelty of golden midwinter light.

When we were told that spring soccer for the children started in February Terry and I looked at each other and rolled our eyes. Cruelty, we thought. They'd freeze. February came, and with it a spell of temperatures in the seventies. Soccer practice began. I arrived early to pick up my sons, wriggled my hose off in the privacy of the car, and got out to bask in the sun.

A neighbor knocked on the door one day, holding out a potted plant. "I wanted to be the one to bring you your first azalea!" she exclaimed.

I accepted, grateful enough, but never imagined that in Wilmington you would remember your first azalea forever—and the person who brought it, too. In Maryland azaleas hadn't bloomed until May and had never grown very big—

pretty enough, but such little, squatty things. There was some sort of azalea festival in Wilmington, I knew, which meant they must do well here. But if anyone had told me that in my own garden azaleas would one day grow as big as a man, I wouldn't have believed it for a second.

Every Northerner knows that spring is a tease. You long for it in March, and if you're lucky it arrives by May. The light rises, but not the temperature. The lingering sunsets mock you. Your heat bill is depressing.

Not so in Wilmington. Here the daffodils bloomed the first of March, the days continued to warm (though March winds could be daunting at a soccer game), the end of the month was marked by a sprinkling of tulips.

Then April came, and we learned that the upcoming "Azalea Festival" was a grander event than we'd anticipated. Even our daughter was to be part of it—an Azalea Belle, due to the kindness of yet another neighbor who sponsored her. We rented a fancy hoop-skirted dress for the occasion, from a dressmaker who took her role far too seriously, and we decided the whole affair was pretty silly when—behold!—every flowering tree and shrub in town burst into sudden, dazzling blossom. All this in a matter of days, when in the North the blooming season spreads itself out for months. This was SPRING, in capital letters. This was what all the fuss was about. This was quite something.

Our daughter's responsibility as an Azalea Belle was to grace some of the gardens on the tour, which meant standing around in her costume with other Belles, being decorative. She is fiercely feminist, usually, but she was in need of a wider social life that spring and enjoyed it. I visited each of the gardens she was assigned to, and I was impressed by each one, with its hundreds of plants carefully tended for the past year or more. But what I will always remember is walking back to my car after visiting one of her official posts and seeing a handmade sign in front of another house reading, "Garden open. Come in."

A path led around back, and a number of people were following it, so I did, too. Once behind the house we all stopped in unison. We held our breath. We marveled. Wilmington is mostly flat, but this yard was hilly, punctuated by two streams, wooden bridges leading over them along graceful, winding paths. From a distance the Yoshino cherry trees beckoned to us with arms of pale blossoms, the dogwoods with elegant drifts of white. As far as the eye could see, the banks were covered with azaleas in every shade of pink and purple and white, set against a palette of azure sky and emerald grass. Two older women were walking in front of me, obviously visitors to the area. Like me, for a time they were awestruck, and didn't speak. Then one of them turned to the other and said, "This must be what heaven looks like."

And judging from our first months in Wilmington, the kindnesses we encountered and the splendid climate, the sheer grace of our new hometown and how it has lived up to its promise in all the years since, it certainly is.

In summer I haven't worn pantyhose for years.

Ellyn Bache's novel Safe Passages *was made into a 1995 movie starring Susan Sarandon and Sam Shepard, which she says was nice, but not nearly as nice as moving to Wilmington in 1985. Her other books include the novel* Festival in Fire Season; *a collection of short stories,* The Value of Kindness; *and a nonfiction work,* Culture Clash.

DAPHNE ATHAS

· ·

Right Here

My father heard that Chapel Hill was the

"Athens of the South" from a philosophy professor he'd met in Pigeon Cove, Massachusetts. The word *Athens* attracted him. He was a Greek immigrant who'd escaped a restaurant career, working his way through Ohio University and Harvard Law School to become a Boston stockbroker just in time to get wiped out in 1929. My mother's family were New Englanders dating back to the 1630s. We'd been living in a twelve-bedroom house on the ocean in Gloucester, Massachusetts, where at night we could see the Portland steamer floating by like a lighted birthday cake. The bank thought we could afford to pay the mortgage on our house, so it let us stay more than five years before foreclosing. There were four of us by then, three girls and a boy.

Eastern Point in Gloucester was a peninsula of summer estates. In the winter the

161

millionaires left, but we had to stay. We went to East Gloucester Primary School every day, where our classmates were the Italian, Finnish, Portuguese, and Irish children of fish factory workers. They said "youse guys" and "don't gimme none of them things" and were rough, so we were afraid of them. About the only children we played with were the Nottmans' caretaker's son and the four Birdseye children. Mostly we wandered the Point by ourselves. We picked driftwood daily on the beach to burn in the fireplace to save heat. We sneaked into the deserted estates, took possession, followed the leader on snowy sea walls, and couldn't imagine a world past the ocean's horizon.

When we came to Chapel Hill we didn't have enough rent money to live in a regular white residential neighborhood, so we found a shack for eighteen dollars a month, and my father started a linen supply business on a bicycle. He ordered the denim by mail. Our shack stood on a knoll at the edge of the "colored section" across from the power plant, where the railroad track from Carrboro crossed and Merritt Mill Road turned to dirt. It is now called Knolls Development.

At school Miss Riddle, the civics teacher, said, "Turn to page one hundred and fifty-fo'." Richard Lewis opened his mouth and said undecipherable words. He came from Alabama, his mother was a Playmaker, and Molly Holmes, the brightest and most beautiful girl in the school, was in love with him, which meant he was desirable.

I knew accents; my father had one. The first time I had noticed was when I was nine years old and he was shaving in the bathroom at the end of the long hall in Gloucester, standing with a beard of white lather, his single-bladed razor shining dangerously in the sun. "Come eean," he said. I didn't move, so he repeated it. "You say *in* wrong," I told him. "What is the right way then?" "*In*. Ih, ih," I said, accentuating the short *i* relentlessly. He lifted his lips with effort and imitated me. "Come in," he said correctly. With that one short *i* his authority was demolished and he became ordinary. Fortunately he couldn't keep it up and soon regressed to his autocratic long *e*.

Southern accents meant something, even though I didn't know what. They had a secret logic of their own, the opposite of my sister's when she first saw a public drinking fountain labeled "Colored" and expected the water to be pink. Gradually I figured it out through synesthesia. The "best" clique of girls (professors' children) with their lipstick, pinned sweaters, and cooing open vowels ("You must wah-eer it some-time," after a compliment, a shocking invitation to wear somebody else's clothes that seemed at first either patronizing or insulting), equated with bursting magnolia blossoms, azaleas, and japonica. The merchants' children, knowing what the clerk says when you leave the dime store ("Come back and see us sometime"), equated with judas, dogwood, and pine. "Truck kids," Carrboro mill workers' and farmers' children who said "ditn't" for "didn't," were red clay, chinaberry trees, broom grass, and plug tobacco.

There were no blacks in our school, but at night there was unfamiliar music around us; we heard it from our shack, the strum of sweet guitars, punctuated with screams and hooting laughter said to stem from heat, drink, and razor fights. By day we passed their dark faces on our scorching dusty road, transformed from hidden mystery to something visible but intensely foreign. We smiled and nodded, but never talked. They looked at us as if they knew a secret about us.

Being defined as Yankees, we took it up like a banner. Hadn't good Yankees like Bronson Alcott, Louisa May's father, and Henry James's two younger brothers come to seek their fortunes with carpetbags? Our mother actually owned a carpetbag. It had belonged to her father when he was young. So we hung it on the tongue-and-groove wall to cover a hole, and marshaling the tatters of our pride we told the story of ourselves to the kids in school, how we'd lost everything and lived in a shack. We completed our transvaluation of values: good into bad, bad good, beautiful ugly, ugly beautiful, etc., and invited them over to look at how we'd improvised a Byzantine tent from our hellhole. They saw our piano, tipsy on our rotting floor, our tapestries plugging cracks in the dingy wall, our bookcases of Dickens, Scott, and Greek lexicons. They looked at how we stretched remnant-goods curtains to make ourselves separate rooms. We boasted how we tore rotting boards from the decrepit old barn out back to burn in our crumbling fireplaces. They thought it was wonderful. Even though we were too peculiar to be popular, this agony aside, we became Chapel Hillians.

What better place for such a passage? Only in a town of ideals as self-mythologizing, witty, family oriented, sophisticated, plebeian, Southern, self-deprecating, and attentive to its own heart would it have been possible.

Actually the philosopher had called it the "Athens in the Sahara of the South." I saw the word *Sahara* recently in an old newspaper in the North Carolina Collection at Wilson Library and laughed out loud, for in 1939 the gentry of Chapel Hill behaved as if North Carolina was a seeding ground, not a Sahara. With understated kindliness they let us know they were as cosmopolitan as Europe, and that the Civil War defeat and the state's being the vale of humility between two mountains of conceit (South Carolina and Virginia) had given them the moral imperative to lead the South out of Reconstruction into the twentieth century.

The idea of a college means a place where young people leave home for the first time to meet each other and learn the world through books and argument. In 1940 the University of North Carolina had no medical school, no suburbia, no 15/501 or I-40. There were only three thousand students, mostly in arts, science, and sociology. Horace Williams had led to Paul Green, Professor Koch, the folk movement, Howard Odum, and the Institute for Social Research. Franklin Roosevelt as president was actually translating the progressive social ideas of these educators into reality.

At that time no girls were allowed into the university before their junior year. The "best" girls were usually sent to Salem, Sweet Briar, or some two-year college before coming to finish out their last two years in Chapel Hill. Then in 1940 Orange County girls were allowed in as freshmen for the first time. A society of book-hungry town kids gravitated toward each other as the campus was taken over by navy V-12 and preflight school. It was a strange time for students, as the normal flow of life as they had known it was interrupted by World War II.

In addition to life being turned topsy-turvy in Chapel Hill at the time, a thing called respectability was subtly being redefined. There were Nancy and Mary Smith, Yankees like us. Their mother, Betty Smith, was a Playmaker, divorced and living with a man. Divorce was shameful and exotic. Richard Phillips's father from Georgia was also divorced. He was an editor at UNC Press and Dick was going to be a doctor. Walter Carroll was an orphan brought up by his older sister Loretto, a radical whose plays *Strike* and *Job's Kinfolk* about Gastonia mill workers had been taken to New York by the Playmakers. She'd gotten married and had a baby, so he moved into the house on Macaulay Street with Dick and his father.

Wayne Williams was a Carrboro maverick whose parents weren't divorced but hadn't gone past eighth grade. One dusty dog day of summer Wayne told how when he was about to move over to Chapel Hill High from Carrboro's eighth grade, his teacher said, "Rah-cheer is Carrboro. Next year you're going to a place where kids' fathers are professors and have been to Europe. In Chapel Hill they know more than you, so you'll have to sink or swim." I criticized Wayne for saying "here" as "cheer." He led me to the windows of the abandoned mill (now Carr Mill Mall) and described the deafening noise of the machines where his mother had worked. We walked the railroad track to get to each other's houses, and we talked about God. He blamed me for making him lose his faith. He'd been saved in Carrboro Baptist Church when he was nine or ten.

Horace Williams owned the mill house where Wayne had grown up, and Wayne told me that when the old philosopher was a youth near Dismal Swamp the Methodist church had collected enough money to send him to the University of North Carolina, where he learned Socrates and the art of dialogue. Horace Williams was called Vergil Weldon in Thomas Wolfe's *Look Homeward, Angel*. In real life Wayne used to take the fourteen dollars in rent to Williams every month and look longingly through the screen door at his books. Wily old Horace with his bald dome and reputation as a skinflint once told him maybe they were cousins, since they both had the same last name.

In February Wayne said I should meet Ouida, because in order to understand the South I'd need to see how people dipped snuff, and Ouida's grandmother did it. Ouida was a striking Carrboro girl three years older than Wayne who lived in the next street and who looked after him when he was two or three years old. She greeted us on her grungy porch like a Greenwich Village actress. She had high cheekbones and white skin dusted with freckles, and she wore a snood.

Ouida had no idea of the purpose of our visit, but Wayne wormed us quickly into the hallway, where the old grandmother was huddled over the hot wood stove. Two streams of tobacco juice tracked the wrinkles leading from the corners of her mouth, dyeing them a blackish brown. Wayne declared out loud what we'd come for. "She's a Yankee," he told the old lady. "She's never seen anybody dip snuff." The old woman cackled. Then she got her hickory twig and poked it around her gums and through her dark teeth. After she had done that she arched herself over an empty Campbell's soup can on the floor, wopsed up her mouth, and let go her wad of brown spit. She shook herself during the act as a peacock shakes its feathers, and the sound of the plop echoed. But there was a glint in her eyes which testified to something, some secret that was different from the black people's secret when they saw us in the road.

Ouida had just gotten a job as Paul Green's secretary. Four months earlier her father had left the family on her high-school graduation day, running off with a woman from Raleigh while she waited on the platform in her white dress during "Pomp and Circumstance." She'd had to quit her first semester in college to go to a business school and help the family out.

"I adored him!" she declared later, dramatizing her identity. "If he ever comes back, though, I swear I'll shoot him dead!" Ouida could turn her Southern accent off and on. She could pull her loose "Ah" into a tight "I" sound, the same way she inhaled the drag of her cigarette—she held the smoke in her lungs an eternity, and then she breathed it out with profound gravity. She dated Jews, had a graduate-student boyfriend, and acted as if Carrboro were no stigma.

Wayne and I began consciously to emulate her. We stayed out all hours. We hitchhiked. We spent the night once in the library stacks, deliberately disobeying the cowbell rung by the minion walking his rounds at 11 P.M. We crawled under a graduate carrel and waked up hourly at the bell tower's loud, off-key chime. Wayne got away with it by declaring independence from his mother and father on the grounds of superior education. I got away with it because my father treated me as an adult, free to go to hell in my own handbasket.

As "serious literati" Wayne and I were reaching out to where the real writing was by reading everything we could get our hands on. But it was Ouida who got inside. The dividing line was between the academics who taught and the hardscrabble practitioners who wrote. Paul Green was the master of Chapel Hill's inner sanctum, the man most responsible for getting Faulkner, Clifford Odets, Zora Neale Hurston, Sherwood Anderson, Gertrude Stein, and Richard Wright to town. I used to look at Ouida's orange fingernails and think how amazing that such polish could exist on fingers which were transferring the brains of an American Pulitzer Prize winner to print. Shorthand and typing became elevated in my mind.

At first Ouida didn't tell us much about who she met and what she did. Unbeknownst to Wayne and me, when Clifford Odets came to town—at the height of his fame, the proletarian author of *Golden Boy* and *Awake and Sing*— he took a fancy to Ouida. He wrote in his journal about Ouida's "poor house" where her "mother refused to come in and meet me because her hair wasn't done up right." But when Richard Wright came to collaborate with Paul Green on the play version of *Native Son*, Ouida confided in us about how she invited "Richard" to her house when the last act of the play was written and typed. She told us about how thugs had gotten wind of the invitation and threatened Wright with his life. The next day Wright left town. Ahead of her time, Ouida embodied that driving change in wartime when the demotic and the dangerous were conquering the accepted and the respectable and a different world was being born.

Chapel Hill had grown its own vocabulary, a type of language peculiar to itself and not defined, not even yet. It is Southern lyricism spawned by the play dialogue of the thirties, a pretend-redneck argot which disguises intellect and goes in for sophisticated wit, sociological words, Wolfeian rhapsody, cracker jokes, English poetry, Protestant verse and response, and black gospel. It is high in the guise of low, repetitive ascending syllables that make your hair stand on end.

My friend, Miranda Cambanis, a poet, told me that once in an earthquake when she was a girl in Greece, the people of the island left their toppling houses, afraid of being killed. They went down to the shore trying to escape in boats. But the sea was boiling, they were afraid to go out into it. It bubbled like soup in a cauldron. They sat down and waited. After it was over people were never the same again, even though the stones had not turned color.

Chapel Hill was a crucible like that. Nobody launched inside it could know what the changes would be over the years. The night after visiting Ouida's grandmother I went home and tried to spit a bull's-eye too. Got an old bean soup can out of the garbage and set it on the floor beside the wood stove. Five times I spat. Five times I missed. I ratiocinated it was because I was a foot and a half taller, but that was beside the point. The plop was echoed, the old woman's cornflower-blue eyes glittered above her Cherokee cheeks all these years because she shared with us a North Carolina gallantry. Half generosity, half contempt—the pride of prowess necessary to transform things.

Born in Cambridge, Massachusetts, of a Greek immigrant who boasted of his descent from Zeus and a New Englander whose ancestors came over on the May-flower, **Daphne Athas** *is a hybrid. Her fate was sealed when she arrived in Chapel Hill during adolescence and first experienced the South, at which time she became a "Gulliver of the Piedmont." She has written fiction, nonfiction, poems, plays and essays.*

LOUIS D. RUBIN, JR.

· ·

On Being a North Carolinian

At Hollins College in Virginia, where I

taught for ten years, the admissions office

used to have a rule that if a prospective student was from North Carolina or Texas, at some point during her interview it was mandatory to ask whether she intended to stay at Hollins for four years and to graduate.

This was because, in North Carolina and Texas alone of the Southern states, parents wished their daughters to go to a Virginia women's college for a year or two and get properly cultivated, but then to transfer to the state university, where the odds were considerably better for meeting and marrying boys from the home state.

With girls from Virginia, South Carolina, or any other state, whether Southern, Northeastern, or Midwestern, marrying close to home didn't seem to be a major consideration. But it was important to find out the long-range intentions of the North Carolina and Texas girls, and to shape admission preferences accordingly, if the college's attrition rate was to be kept down so that enrollment in the upper-level classes was not cruelly depleted.

North Carolina, as I found out when I moved to Chapel Hill to teach more than half an adult lifetime ago, was—and largely still is—very much a locally centered kind of place. One word for this is *provincial*. Another is *self-sufficient*. Whichever is appropriate—perhaps both are—what matters is that people in North Carolina do not tend to regulate themselves by what goes on elsewhere. The point of view isn't primarily national or even regional, not *inter*-but *intra*-state.

Unlike its neighboring states to the north and south, North Carolina wasn't peopled from the seacoast. Settlers didn't arrive from the sea and push westward. Instead, a majority of the early North Carolinians first came down from coastal Virginia, then up from Low Country South Carolina, then down from the middle colonies via the Valley of Virginia. Once in place, they mostly stayed put.

Growing up as I did in Charleston, and then moving to Richmond with my family, the only part of North Carolina that I saw when young lay along the railroad corridors. Then during the war, while in the army, I discovered the novels of Thomas Wolfe. I was enthralled. The vicissitudes and triumphs of Wolfe's autobiographical spokesman Eugene Gant in the thinly camouflaged confines of Asheville, and during Eugene's years at the even more transparently depicted university town known as Pulpit Hill in the state of Old Catawba, set me to vibrating sympathetically as no book had ever done before then (or, for that matter, since then).

I resolved to take my remaining year of college at Chapel Hill, and while still in the army I went through the preliminary steps of applying for admission. But when I was discharged early in 1946, there wasn't time enough to do anything other than finish up at the University of Richmond.

So I didn't follow in my Tar Heel literary hero's footsteps, and, in point of fact, during the ensuing two decades I never even once so much as set foot upon the campus where Eugene Gant had once bounded along the pathways at night uttering wild goat-cries.

Then, while on sabbatical leave from Hollins College, I was invited to spend the spring 1965 term in Chapel Hill as visiting professor, and two years later I accepted a permanent appointment. Thus, in the fall of 1967, I found myself installed in Thomas Wolfe's Pulpit Hill in Old Catawba—though I'd long since gone on to admire other and more complex writers.

Living in North Carolina took a little getting used to. There is an old pleasantry to the effect that the state is "a vale of humility between two mountains of conceit"—i.e., South Carolina and Virginia—but in some ways a mountain range of humility seemed more like it. The "just plain old Tar Heel folks" bit tended to be laid on thickly. Especially in Chapel Hill, the self-proclaimed "Southern Part of Heaven," a self-congratulatory motif was omnipresent.

Having grown up in Charleston and lived in Richmond, it wasn't as if I hadn't previously been exposed to heavy doses of civic self-praise. My initial response was to view the North Carolina variety as more of the same, with perhaps even less historical excuse for it.

What I began to realize after a time, however, was that whatever form such communal narcissism might take elsewhere, in Chapel Hill and North Carolina neither smug complacency nor undue self-importance was involved. There was nothing, or very little, that was vain or bovine about the state of North Carolina. It could be wrong-headed, it could even be willfully blind to actualities; but vainglorious it wasn't. However often joked about, the humility was genuine.

I came to feel, and after several decades continue to feel, that compared with the people of any other place where I have lived, there is less pretense, less "side" to the citizenry of North Carolina. Hauteur and clannishness are equally alien to their makeup. Class and social distinctions there are, but they don't seem particularly relevant to the way that things work. People in North

Carolina don't ordinarily get elected to high office on the basis of a family name. The state is conservative; it is not hidebound.

More like the Midwest than the South, perhaps? No, not really. There isn't that sense of sameness, of dour conformity, that I have felt in comparable surroundings north of the Ohio River and west of the Alleghenies. There is a role for eccentricity, color, gaudiness. Significantly, where the Midwestern writers whose works I taught in my American literature classes had fled their home states for the East, for Europe, for elsewhere, the North Carolina writers—Thomas Wolfe being the notable exception—have tended to stay and work in North Carolina.

I have the sense, in North Carolina, of there being notably less looking down socially upon other people than elsewhere in the South. Perhaps this is due to the absence of a formidable heritage of aristocratic rule; a wealthy planter class never exercised decisive control over the state government in the early days. If there is an Establishment—where isn't there one?—the possession of an elaborate family tree with roots going back to colonial and early national times isn't a major criterion for membership in it. Thus, the effort to gain or to protect lofty social status as such isn't as important in the scheme of things as in nearby states. Compared to the deadly earnest debutante strategy taking place each winter in Richmond, Norfolk, Charleston, etc., an air of the comically absurd hovers about the annual Terpsichorean Ball in Raleigh.

This is not to say, however, that state pride and civic self-esteem are negligible factors in what makes the citizenry behave. On the contrary, I noticed very quickly that the inhabitants clearly consider anyone who is wise enough to live in North Carolina to be, by definition, privileged. In a sense, the state of North Carolina is one huge booster club.

Now, by this, I certainly do not wish to imply that residence in either South Carolina or Virginia does not also involve considerable hubris. No indeed; if not mountains of self-approbation, as the saying has it, the states to North Carolina's north and south are thoroughly convinced of their superior virtues. The difference is that your Charlestonian, for example, not only feels grateful to heaven for having set him or her down there to enjoy life in the "Holy City," but also assumes without question that all who dwell anywhere else are duly bound to acknowledge their comparative inferiority.

Similarly, if anyone is so abysmally blind as not to be aware of the grandeur of residence in the Commonwealth of Virginia (*Sic semper tyrannis*), so uneducated and uninformed a human being couldn't possibly count for anything—except perhaps somewhere like North Carolina or, even worse, West Virginia. There is no need for a Virginian or a South Carolinian to advertise superiority of status; as well expect a saint to gild his or her halo.

The Tar Heel, by contrast, is eager to cite the merits of his home state; there will be no need to coax him into enumerating its advantages. It isn't that he wishes to boast, mind you, and still less that he is on the defensive about it. There is simply so much satisfaction involved in living in North Carolina that he can't help commenting on it, whether to outsiders or—more characteristically—to fellow Tar Heels.

Recently, the state government produced a television commercial proclaiming musically that "North Carolina is my home!" while displaying various scenic and civic attractions. It was designed to be shown not over out-of-state stations, with an eye toward encouraging tourism. Oh no. It was for within North Carolina itself, for the edification of the state's own residents, in much the same way that Edwardian Englishmen used to take satisfaction in singing "Land of Hope and Glory."

A few years after I moved to North Carolina from Virginia, in the early 1970s, I was asked to put together a program about literature for a delegation of *Time, Life*, and *Fortune* editors who would be spending several days in the Chapel Hill–Raleigh–Durham area as part of the Time-Life empire's effort to remind its executives that civilization also existed, in however rudimentary form, out in the provinces.

In my introductory remarks, I sought to help the visiting editors understand the difference between North Carolina and Virginia. If you go driving along a highway in Virginia, I explained, you will pass a historical marker every mile or so, and it will describe the doings of George Washington, Thomas Jefferson, James Madison, James Monroe, John Marshall, Patrick Henry, Booker T. Washington, Robert E. Lee, Stonewall Jackson, Captain John Smith, and the like. If you go driving along a highway in North Carolina, you will likewise encounter a historical marker every mile or so, but you will never have heard of any of the people named on the markers.

My point was not that the North Carolinians thus honored were unworthy of being commemorated on roadside markers. Rather, it was that in selecting who and what were to be cited on highway signs, the authorities in North Carolina didn't *care* whether or not their choices were renowned elsewhere. Their importance in and to North Carolina was what mattered. Like the television commercial, the historical markers weren't placed there for the tourists, but to be read by the local citizenry.

As an author of books, I have noticed an interesting and, I think, characteristic difference between North Carolina and her neighboring states to the north and south. When a resident of Virginia brings out a new book, it will doubtless get reviewed in the newspaper in the city nearest to the author's place of residence, but the newspapers elsewhere in Virginia feel no obligation to notice it. The same is largely true in South Carolina. But in North Carolina, if a resident of, say, Winston-Salem publishes a new book, it will very likely be reviewed not only there but in Asheville, Charlotte, Greensboro, Durham, Raleigh, Fayetteville, and probably Wilmington—in, that is, any daily newspaper in North Carolina that habitually devotes review space to new books.

It is possible, I suppose, to view that kind of thing as the expression of a pervasive self-consciousness and sense of inferiority. Simple *pride of state* is a more likely explanation. In other words, if you are Southern, you tend to establish your own identity at least in part in terms of your native state. Thus, the resident Tar Heel equates his own self-esteem with that of North Carolina and, like the rooster, feels entitled to crow lustily whenever one of the hens in his coop lays an egg.

There remains, for me, the matter of personal affiliation. Where do I come in?

By virtue of extensive residence in South Carolina and Virginia, I can claim reasonably firsthand experience of those two Southeastern states. I have written three novels set in the city of Charleston, South Carolina, and I wrote a history of Virginia in the *States and the Nation* series during the country's bicentennial celebration. About North Carolina I have written comparatively little, but I have lived here for thirty years—for considerably longer, as an adult, than anyplace else.

I have wondered sometimes which of the three states I ought to consider myself as attached to most powerfully. Not Virginia, certainly; for though I admire the state and spent the best ten years of my life at Hollins College, I never thought of myself as a Virginian.

As for South Carolina, there is no question that being born and growing up in Charleston was the experience that has exerted the greatest formative impact upon my imagination—on the way that I think and feel. When seated at a table or listening to a lecture or attending a meeting, and doodling with pencil on paper, I often find myself writing the letters *S.C.*, but never *N.C.* or *Va.* Nor have I ever been able to write fiction set anywhere else, for fiction involves emotion as well as thought, and Charleston, South Carolina, is the only place where, as I writer, I know how things *feel*.

Yet the Charleston that I know is the one that existed a half-century or more ago, not the present city. When I go there—and I have done so several times a year ever since leaving in 1942—I am little more than a tourist, for almost all the people I knew there are dead or else have long since moved away. When I go to Charleston now, it is like stepping onto the stage of a theater in which the scenery and props for a familiar play are still in place but the actors are missing. So, insofar as being alive and active in a time and place is concerned, as the television commercial puts it, North Carolina is *my* home, too.

For almost all my life, first by birth and rearing, then by conscious choice, I have lived in the South. It has its considerable faults, all right, but I've never been anywhere that I liked nearly so well. I like the hot summers, the short winters, the protracted, long-lingering springs and falls. I like the way people behave in the South, and the way they get along with each other. I like the consciousness of history, the abiding sense of the comic, the reliance upon good manners up and down the line.

North Carolina is very much a *Southern* state. There is more of what I like about the South, and less of what I dislike about it, present in the state of North Carolina than anywhere else I have ever lived. When I'm driving along a highway in a far-distant state somewhere and I see another car with a North Carolina license plate ("First in Flight"), my heart leaps up. As was said of a different Southern place in Spencer Williams's "Beale Street Blues," I'd rather be there than anyplace I know.

Louis D. Rubin, Jr., lives in Chapel Hill, taught at the university there for twenty-three years, founded Algonquin Books of Chapel Hill and headed it for ten years. He now writes and paints. His most recent books are a novel, The Heat of the Sun; *a reference work,* A Writer's Companion; *and a book of essays,* Babe Ruth's Ghost and Other Literary and Historical Speculations.